Last Minute Speeches and Toasts

By
Andrew Frothingham

CAREER
PRESS
Franklin Lakes, NJ

LAST MINUTE SPEECHES AND TOASTS
Cover design by Foster & Foster
Typesetting by Eileen Munson
Printed in the U.S.A. by Book-mart Press

To order this title, please call toll-free 1-800-CAREER-1 (NJ and Canada: 201-848-0310) to order using VISA or MasterCard, or for further information on books from Career Press.

CAREER
PRESS

The Career Press, Inc., 3 Tice Road, PO Box 687, Franklin Lakes, NJ 07417
www.careerpress.com

Library of Congress Cataloging-in-Publication Data
Frothingham, Andrew.
  Last minute speeches and toasts / by Andrew Frothingham.
    p. cm.
  Includes index.
  ISBN 1-56414-493-3 (paper)
    1. Speeches, addresses, etc. 2. Toasts. 3. Speechwriting.
  I. Title

PN6122 .F723 2000
808.5'1—dc21   00-050712

This book is dedicated to

my two sons

in the hope that

they may become

speakers.

Table of Contents

Part II: Gems You Can Use

Introduction

You are scheduled to say a few words in public in the very near future. You are probably nervous. Maybe you are even panicking. Possibly you are starting to think of faking laryngitis. Relax. You are holding the book that will make things better. Once you have the right perspective, know a few tricks of speaking, and have found a good line or two, things will seem a lot less challenging.

Here are five secrets of speaking you should know:

Last minute speaking is a golden opportunity.

When you get asked to speak at the last minute, it's a no lose situation. People are grateful that you are willing to fill in, and expectations are lower than if you had weeks to prepare.

Many people do their best speaking when they have less time to prepare. Their comments are less rehearsed and sound more spontaneous. Their ideas sound fresher. The adrenaline that surges through their bodies when they face a challenge without extensive preparation gives them extra energy.

Last minute speaking is now the norm.

A few decades ago, speaking was a more practiced art form, and speakers often devoted great amounts of time to preparing and rehearsing. No more. Today, everyone is so busy that speeches almost always get prepared at the last minute.

You can stray from the topic.

If you are asked to speak on a specific topic, you don't have to speak only about that topic. If you are a football coach, speak about football, no matter what the topic. Acknowledge the assigned topic, then move on to the topic that you have the most to say about.

Your grammar doesn't have to be perfect.

The standards for speaking are very different from the standards for writing. When you speak, you are expected to sound like you are talking, not as if you are reading. Feel free to use sentence fragments...*isn't* instead of *is not*...even a little slang. Whatever works. Once you realize that you can let go and be yourself, you are likely to give a better speech.

You don't have to fill the whole time slot.

It's rarely a problem if you use less than the amount of time assigned to your speech. If you finish up a bit early, people may have time for a more leisurely meal, more time to network, or get to beat the traffic. None of these are bad things.

If, on the other hand, you go over your time allowance, you can throw off a whole day's schedule. Other people may not have time for their presentations. Meals may be rushed or overcooked. Overtime charges may be incurred for the room, audiovisual (AV) staff, security guards, and who knows what else.

Even when professionals take months preparing speeches, they almost never use all the time they could. When in doubt, keep things short. Length does not make a speech memorable or effective. Abraham Lincoln's Gettysburg Address was only 269 words, but it is one of the great speeches of all time.

There's lots more that could be said, but you're in a rush. So dive into this book and get the advice and material you need to be a star.

Part I:
About
Speaking

How to Use
This Book

If you have time, read the relevant section of Part I to get some tips on speaking.

If, however, you are in a super-rush, go straight to Part II and skim the category that best describes the occasion at which you will be speaking. In most cases, the right category will be obvious. If you are speaking at a reunion, go to Reunions (page 126). If you are speaking at the dedication of a library, go to Library (page 101).

In some cases, you may have to be a little creative. If you are speaking at a party in celebration of a divorce (a rare kind of party, so we haven't made it a category), you could go to Weddings (page 154) and find a quote to disagree with. You could also find a joke in Dispute (page 70) to use.

You should try to find three gems you like and use them at the beginning, middle, and end of your speech. If you can find only one gem you like for the occasion, use it at the beginning, and end your speech with the biggest, most sincere "thank you" you can muster.

How to Choose and Use Quotes

Using a quote can add authority to almost any point that you are making. However, a quote only helps if it is both relevant to what you're saying and appropriate to your audience.

That does not mean the quote has to be perfectly on point. You can often use a quote on the right topic, but which expresses the wrong point of view. We once wrote a speech for the head of a sales force that began:

"I've been thinking about Alfred Lord Tennyson's famous lines about the Charge of the Light Brigade:

'Theirs not to make reply,
Theirs not to reason why,
Theirs but to do and die.'

I realized that this is the dumbest set of orders I've ever heard.

It's no wonder the Light Brigade got slaughtered. My charge to you is the exact opposite. I want you to reason why—and I want you to live and thrive, not die."

Some pointers when using quotes

» Use quotes to reinforce your message, not to show off your knowledge.

» Quote people whose names the audience is likely to recognize. The quotes in this book come, for the most part, from well-known people. There are many wonderful quotes from obscure people, but the odds are you don't have time to learn who they are or to explain who they are to your audience.

» Name the author only if you know how to pronounce his or her name. You can always introduce the quote with a phrase like "An author once wrote..." or "It's been said that...."

» Use the shorter version of a name when possible. It's fine to say Mark Twain without adding that his real name was Samuel Longhorne Clemens. Use one name if that's how an author is best known. Say "Milton," rather than John Milton, and "Shakespeare," rather than "William Shakespeare."

» Mention the date of the quote only when it makes the quote more meaningful. For people who think that temperance is a new fad, it's interesting that the phrase "Moderation in all things" was said by Terrence in the 2nd century BC. On the other hand, the fact that Charles M. Schultz came up with the book title *Happiness Is a Warm Puppy* in 1962 doesn't add much. For this reason, we've included dates after only a few names.

» Quote accurately. Even if you abbreviate your own notes, it is still a good idea to write out any quotes in full.

The 3-Step Fail-Safe Structure for a Speech

Ask salespeople to name the "3 Ts" and they will recite:

> Tell 'em what you're going to tell 'em;

> Tell 'em;

> Tell 'em what you told 'em.

This structure works as well in speeches as it does in sales pitches.

In speeches, repetition is not only okay, it's good. A speech is very different from a book. Because a listener can't go back and review, it's important that you repeat your main points.

In the first part of your speech, tell the audience your major points in outline form. ("Tell 'em what you're going to tell 'em.")

In the middle part of your speech, repeat your points, filling them out. ("Tell 'em.")

At the end of your speech, say the points again. Announce that you are repeating, or recapping, or summarizing, so the audience doesn't think you are making a mistake ("Tell 'em what you told 'em."), but don't skip this step.

In emergencies, such as when the speaker before you uses up too much time and you get cut short, you can go straight to your wrap-up, the "tell 'em what you told 'em" part, and still get your points across.

The 3-T structure works like a charm. It makes it easy for your audience to follow, and believe, what you say.

Stick to 4 Points

One of the biggest mistakes speakers make is trying to say too much. That's understandable: A speech is a golden opportunity, so you want to say all you can. The problem is, the more points you make, the less likely the audience is to remember what you say. It's much better to limit yourself to four points and hammer them home. Ideally, the first two or three points should add up to make your last point seem almost inevitable.

The rule of sticking to four points applies to the question-and-answer session, if there is one, too. Answer only the questions that have to do with your four points. If a questioner wants you to talk about anything else, offer to discuss his or her question one-on-one after the group session.

~~~

5 Killer Opening Strategies

The first few minutes of a speech are the most important. That's when you need to grab the audience's attention. Here are five strategies that work well:

1. Compliment the audience.

People like to hear about themselves. One speaker I know starts her speeches by saying, "Wow, you are great." You may want to find a more clever way of saying this.

One great opening line for an emcee (MC), used by British speakers and later borrowed by an American president, is, "Being the MC here is like being the corpse at a wake. You can't start without me, but I'm not expected to do very much." I had a client who felt that this opener was too morbid, so we came up with "Being the MC here is like throwing out the first pitch on the opening day of the baseball season. I appreciate the honor, but I know that the real stars are the ones who will stand up when I sit down."

The next year, the same client wanted to say the same thing, only differently, so we suggested the line, "I feel like a referee at a pro basketball game. I am surrounded by giants."

2. Offer valuable information or opportunities.

People watch half-hour-long infomercials because they think they are going to get valuable information. The same motivation will get them to listen to you. We heard an executive start a speech saying, "I'm going to tell you what you have to do to get promoted and what you have to do to win bonuses." Everyone in the room paid attention.

Even if you can't promise to make people rich, you can often promise a chance for them to be known and remembered as someone who made a big difference in many lives. Or you may be able to promise people a chance for a once-in-a-lifetime experience.

3. Put the audience in a state of suspense.

If you start a speech by saying you'd like to give two cheers to a person, company, community, and so forth, your audience will pay attention so they can find out why you aren't satisfied enough to give three cheers. This is a great way to set up a speech in which you offer a few compliments, but challenge people to do better.

4. Scare the audience.

Preachers have long known that describing the terrors of hell can be more compelling than describing the pleasures of heaven. You may not want to preach fire and brimstone, but you can often catch an audience by describing what could befall the country, the community, the company, or an individual if the people in the audience don't heed your words.

Freshman orientation at many colleges starts with this kind of sobering thought: "Look at the two people to your left, and the two people to your right. The odds are one of them will not be here in four years."

5. Break the protocol.

Speeches are like ballet or opera. Audiences have strong expectations for how you will act. If you break the protocol, you grab attention. People sense that something unusual is happening.

One speaker we know likes to use a wireless microphone so he can start his speeches from the back of the room or even from the middle of the audience. Another likes to kick over the lectern and prowl around the front of the stage. A calmer speaker we know simply enters the audience to pay a friend a dollar he owes him.

6 Last Minute Resources

Even when you have totally blown it, have no time to do research, and your Internet connection is down, here are a few resources you can turn to (above and beyond this book, which will, almost always, do the trick).

Of course, if your Internet connection isn't down, you should have no problem finding great facts and quotes to add to your talk.

In addition, if you are comfortable quoting from the Bible, and if it is appropriate to quote the Bible to your audience, bibles are easy to find (thanks to the Gideon Society). Open to almost any page and you'll find an interesting passage.

1. The meeting invitation or program

Scour the invitation and program. You are bound to find something in them. Can you comment on whether the title of the meeting would have made sense 20 years ago? Are you honored to be following a particular speaker or on the same program with a particular expert? Can you comment about the city where the meeting is being held? We once heard a speaker start a speech in a hotel with the word sand in its name. He described how sand could be viewed as useless, but how people with vision can see that it contains silica, which could make glass or even silicon chips.

2. The dictionary

This is the oldest speaking trick there is, but it still works. If your topic is "Responsibility," and you find in your dictionary (*The Random House Dictionary of the English Language, Second Edition, Unabridged*, [New York: Random House, 1987] in this case) that the third definition is "a particular burden of obligation upon one who is responsible," you have a place to start. Read that definition and then go on to say that you think of responsibility as a pleasure rather than a burden.

Most hotels have a dictionary in the business office. Ask to borrow it.

3. The weather page or the weather channel

Get up and say, "Today, the high temperature for the nation is [x] in [city] and the low is [y] in [city], which makes me pretty happy to be here. It also makes me think that if people can tolerate that range of temperatures, they ought to be able to...."

4. Fortune cookies

Find the nearest Chinese restaurant and buy one or two dozen fortune cookies. Open them all and read the fortunes. Choose one or two to open with. If you get one that says, "You will soon meet interesting people" or "Good things will happen soon," go on to say that it's true, because you have just met this great audience.

5. The sports page

The sports page is always full of surprise victories, valiant efforts, and comebacks. Often you can get as much material from the losers as the winners. We once heard a speaker begin a speech to a dejected sales force saying, "This morning, the Chicago Cubs are in last place. In the cellar by five games. But do you think anyone on the Cubs has stopped trying? Do you think anyone on the team does not have a dream of how they could claw their way back up to the top? Of course not. They are pros. And so are you."

6. Your family

Your very last resort is to quote your family. Quoting something your late grandmother once said is a safe strategy. Few people are likely to argue with your citation.

A friend of ours captured a crowd by saying, "I'm not sure what I should say to you, but I know what my Uncle J. L. would say. He'd lean back, fix his cold blue eyes on you, and ask, 'Are you fixin' to get hit by the same truck twice?' He wouldn't blame you if someone took advantage of you. But if you let it happen a second time, he had no pity. We've been hurt. Here's what we need to do to make sure it doesn't happen again."

7 Facts That Can Spice Up Almost Any Speech

1. Communicate quickly.

Andrew Jackson's most famous battle, the Battle of New Orleans (January 8, 1815), was fought two weeks after the War of 1812 ended when the Treaty of Ghent was signed in Europe. Thousands died because of slow communications.

2. The experts are often wrong.

A studio executive looking at Fred Astaire's screen test said, "Can't act. Can't sing. Can dance a little." Hollywood producer Darryl Zanuck panned Clark Gable's screen test saying, "His ears are too big. He looks like an ape." Both of the people who were so rudely rejected went on to be big stars.

3. Averages don't matter.

You can drown in a puddle that has an average depth of six inches. Averages don't always tell the whole story. If the puddle is big enough, it could be one-inch deep for most of its surface, and also have a six-foot-deep sink hole. To really know what you are talking about, you have to deal with the most accurate, clearest, and most specific facts you can get.

4. Good works carry far.

The sun is about 93 million miles (150 million kilometers) away from the Earth, but it provides us with virtually all our light, warmth, and energy. You don't have to be on the scene to have a positive impact.

5. Things add up.

A dollar invested at 10 percent interest, compounded annually, almost doubles in seven years, and if the legendary $24 dollars paid for Manhattan in 1624 had been invested at 6 percent, compounded annually, it would be worth over $74 billion today. Every little difference you make today can contribute to changing the future.

6. We are all related.

Current genetic research indicates that all humans now on earth are descended from a few different females. If you are arguing with someone, think about the fact that you may well be arguing with a cousin.

7. It's worth trying.

In baseball, if you only strike out twice for each hit you get, you are hitting .333 and you are considered a batting champ. It doesn't matter if you miss now and then, as long as you are ready to take a swing.

Pro Tips

Have something to say.

Unless you are good looking enough to be on magazine covers, no one is there just to look at you. The audience wants you to have something to say—ideally something you feel strongly about.

If you don't believe what you are saying, your audience certainly won't either. Let them know why you are talking. Tell them why they should care about the topic. If you're giving a sales pitch, don't forget to ask for the order. If you're talking about disaster relief, ask the audience for their prayers, and perhaps their money.

Be yourself.

Dr. Benjamin Spock's legendary advice to parents, "You know more than you think you do," is also good advice to speakers. You know how to speak. You've been in audiences, congregations, or classes. You know what works and what doesn't. Use your common sense and do what is most comfortable.

Forget the fact that you're speaking to a crowd. Imagine you're speaking to a close friend. Use the words that you would normally use, not the big impressive ones you find in the dictionary. If you normally use big gestures, use even bigger ones when you speak.

If you are really comfortable, leave the lectern and walk around. Walk into the audience. Sit on the stage. The more comfortable you are with the audience, the more comfortable they will be with you.

Take control.

The first two minutes of a speech are the moments when you have to grab your audience's attention. Remember: You are talking to people who do most of their viewing and listening with a remote control in their hand, ready to surf past anything that doesn't grab them within six seconds. You have to know your greeting and your first three sentences cold so you can look straight into your audience's eyes as you deliver your opening.

Your greeting is important. If you were personally introduced, start with a short thank you while you are looking toward the person who made the introduction. Don't bother to thank videotaped introductions. Next, with your head up and eyes to the audience, give them a hearty "Good morning" or "Hello there." Don't go for one of those long "Ladies and gentlemen, distinguished guests, esteemed colleagues and brothers in the Distinguished Knighthood of Turtles" openings unless tradition demands it. The point is to establish a dialogue with the audience.

If you want the audience to talk back to you, now's the time to get the process started. If they don't say hello back, clear your throat and say hello again with an expectant look. When you get an answer, say, "That's better."

If you didn't like how you were introduced, correct the introduction in the first five minutes. We saw a speaker catch a fading audience by saying, "I was introduced as the president of a company, but that shouldn't mean anything to you. My real credentials are that I was a field salesman for 20 years. My right arm is longer than my left from carrying a bag. I still have 1,200 mini-bottles of hotel shampoo to go through. The only difference is that now I have to be more careful about my expense reports, to set a good example."

Part of taking control is learning not to apologize. Doctors rarely say, "I don't know how to do this operation, but I'll try." Lawyers rarely say, "I'm not very good in the courtroom, but I'll do my best." For the same reasons, you should never start with "I'm not much of a speaker..." or "Unaccustomed as I am to public speaking...."

Don't panic if things go wrong.

Once you're in control, you should stay in control, no matter what happens. Few speeches are delivered without a hitch, but we've never seen an audience fail to be sympathetic and attentive to a speaker who acknowledges problems as they occur and keeps going.

If, for example, the previous speaker says half of what you were going to say, don't repeat the material. Instead, shorten your speech and refer back to hers: "As Mala has just pointed out, the economy in Asia is dangerously volatile...."

If your speech happens to be scheduled at the same time as a major sporting event that your audience cares about, tell them that you will announce scores at intervals during your speech. You can also offer to end a few minutes early so you can all watch the last few minutes of play together.

Close your speech with a bang, then sit down.

Your close is the last chance to reach your audience; it's the part they're most likely to remember. Make it memorable. After you have "told 'em what you told 'em," end on a strong, positive note.

Try to make your last sentence about the audience. One marketing executive we work with makes it a rule to end every speech to the sales force with a sentence that contains the word *you* at least twice.

President Franklin D. Roosevelt gave this advice about speaking: "Be sincere; be brief; be seated." He was absolutely right. Once you've made your points and closed, say thank you and sit down. If your speech is followed by a question-and-answer session, put a strong closing sentence at the end of your last answer.

Salespeople have a rule that says, "Never talk past the close." In sales situations, it means once the customers have said yes, don't yammer on and give them a chance to change their minds. In speeches it means stop on your strong close, so they remember you as a forceful speaker with a point.

One trick is to handle any housekeeping details before your close. If you are the speaker before lunch, take time at the start of your comments to tell people about the agenda changes for the afternoon, the survey they need to fill out, the donation cards, and the location for lunch before you "tell 'em what you told 'em." This is particularly important if you are using an audiovisual close. You ruin the effect if you stand up after the screens have been full of exploding fireworks and volcanoes and the sound system has blared out a moving crescendo.

Questions to Ask

The more you customize your speech or toast to the audience, the better it will be. People pay attention when they think that you are addressing their specific interests.

That's why you should find out everything you can about your audience before you start thinking about what you will say. Here are just a few of the questions you should ask:

How big is the audience?

If the audience is only five people, you may want to be informal.

Who is the audience?

Are they executives? Are they salespeople? Are they volunteers? Are they intellectuals? Is it a fraternal organization? You will want to speak to people in their own language!

Why are they gathered?

Are they there to learn? Did they elect to attend or is it a required meeting? If attendance is mandatory, don't thank people for coming.

What is the male/female balance?

The sports images and analogies that might work with an all-male audience could fall flat with a mostly female group.

What's the average age?

You may want to use a more respectful tone with an older crowd.

Where are they from?

A speech full of references to baseball rules and clichés might not work with a European audience. A toast that contains a reference to a New York neighborhood may not make much sense to the Andersons from Billings, Montana.

What kind of mood are they in?

If a group is having a winning year, you can congratulate them and then go on to challenge them. If, however, they are having a bad year, you will want to tone things down a bit and be more inspirational.

Where are you on the agenda?

Are you speaking in prime time, or are you part of a sideshow? Are you speaking alone or are you part of a panel? If you are speaking just before lunch, keep it short.

What did they hear at the last meeting?

Did last year's speaker say something that you can build on? Was something said that you don't want to repeat?

What do they expect from you?

If they expect to be inspired, look for inspiring quotes. If they expect to be challenged, look them in the eye and challenge them.

Your Fallback: Speak About Speaking

If you have no expertise about the subject you are asked to speak on and nothing in particular you want to say, but you can't get out of the engagement, the only thing left is to speak about the fact that you are speaking. Luckily, some great things have been said about being a speaker. Here are a few of them:

Quotes about speaking

"I have never seen an ass who talked like a human being, but I have met many human beings who talked like asses."

—Heinrich Heine

"A lecture ought to be something which all can understand, about something which interests everybody."
—Oliver Wendell Holmes

"Every man is eloquent once in his life."
—Ralph Waldo Emerson

"I served with General Washington in the Legislature of Virginia...and...with Doctor Franklin in Congress. I never heard either of them speak 10 minutes at a time, not to any but the main point."
—Thomas Jefferson

"A man never becomes an orator if he has anything to say."
—Finley Peter Dunne

"What orators lack in depth they make up for in length."
—Baron de Montesquieu

"My method is to take the utmost trouble to find the right thing to say, and then to say it with the utmost levity."
—George Bernard Shaw

"Accustomed as I am to public speaking, I know the futility of it."
—Franklin Pierce Adams

Sayings about speaking

A good speech is like a pencil; it has to have a point.

As they say in Texas, speeches are like steer horns—a point here, a point there, and a lot of bull in between.

Public speaking is an audience participation event; if it weren't, it would be private speaking.

Exhaust neither the topic nor the audience.

Caution: Do not open mouth until brain is in gear.

Jokes about speaking

The best after-dinner speech to hear is, "Waiter, I'll take the check, please."

Definition of a great speech? A strong beginning and a great end—preferably close together.

"Sir," the investor began, "I've just read through your speech and I don't have the foggiest idea where you stand on the issue."

"Why thank you very much, my boy," the executive beamed, "do you know how long it took me to get the speech just that way?"

"I have just got a new theory of eternity."
(Comment following a two-hour after-dinner speech)

After speaking for more than two hours without a pause, the professor apologized for going on for so long. "You see, I forgot my watch today," he explained.

"That's okay," replied a student, " there's a calendar in back of you."

Most speakers don't need an introduction—just a conclusion.

"I feel like Liz Taylor's fourth husband: I know what I am supposed to do, but I am at a loss as to how to make it different."

The featured speaker listened with growing amazement as she was described as the greatest speaker on Earth. When it was finally her turn to speak, she said, "After an introduction like that I can hardly wait to hear what I'm going to say."

The Art of Using AV

The more senses you can appeal to, the more effectively you communicate. That's what audiovisual (AV) is all about. When your audience sees something that reinforces the things that you are saying, they are much more likely to get your message.

The other side of that kind of thinking is that an audience gets messages not only from what you show them, but also from how it is shown. Having audiovisual speech support that doesn't work, or that delivers messages that argue with what you are saying, is worse than having no audiovisual support at all.

Keep slides short.

The most common mistake that people make with audiovisual elements is to assume that everyone in the room has perfect 20-20 vision and is an expert speed reader. As a rule, you should never put more information up on a screen than you would put onto a teabag tag or a T-shirt.

A slide that looks like this is a problem:

"Putting full sentences on a slide is almost always a mistake. You are asking the audience to read, when you want them to listen to you. This can be distracting. It is almost always better to abbreviate. Try making an outline of your speech, and then condense things even more"

A better slide would be:
- → Keep slides short.
- → No full sentences.

Don't turn your back on the audience.

When professional speakers use audiovisual support, they insist that things be set up so they can see what they need to see without turning their back on the audience or the camera. Video monitors are often built into the tops of lecterns or into boxes that sit at the front of the stage and face the speaker. TelePrompTers, are positioned so speakers read a script while appearing to look straight into the camera. These speakers know that when you lose eye contact with an audience, you can lose their attention as well. (You know this too: Remember what used to happen in 7th grade when a substitute teacher turned her or his back on the class!)

If you must look at what's on the big screen behind you, turn only halfway and use a quick glance.

Don't rely on your AV.

While AV support can make for a much better speech, you must always be ready to go on without it in case it fails. Speakers used to tell tales of the day the slide bulb burned out or the day the slide tray fell and the slides spilled out. We attended one speech where the speaker had placed glass-packed slides near an air conditioner and every slide developed a distracting puddle of condensed water that changed shape as the slide heated up. Today, speakers are also telling stories about the day the computer froze and all they could project was the screen saver.

Make sure your speech would work for a blind person.

Can the Net.

Even though there are lots of materials on the Internet that you can use to illustrate a speech, never plan on using real-time, live, online Web sites as AV support. Some day soon you may be able to do this, but for the moment, you should assume that you won't be able to get online, that the site will be slow, or that something else will happen to mess up your demonstration.

If you want to use Web-based materials, find a way to "can" it. Use screen shots or some other technology to capture the sites in advance.

The Tricks of Toasting

Toasts and speeches are very much alike; that's why they are both in the title of this book. Toasts have the same relationship to speeches as poetry has to novels. They should be shorter and less complex, but equally moving.

Some occasions call for speeches and not toasts. If there are glasses on the table, however, the chances are that a toast is appropriate.

Once upon a time, toasts were longer. If you read accounts of 18th century banquets, you will find comments about flowery, 20-minute or longer toasts. Don't even think about rambling on for that long. Think of your toast as a commercial. Thirty seconds or so is a nice length. If you go on for much longer, people are likely to put their glasses down or start drinking them.

When you are giving a toast, don't make a big deal out of waiting for complete silence in the room, or waiting for everyone to have perfectly filled glasses. Also, don't make a fuss if someone toasts with a glass of water; it's now considered perfectly appropriate to do so.

Make your toast positive. A toast is meant to be a tribute, not an insult.

Many of the quotes that are found in this book can be used in toasts. Just start out with, "As Shakespeare said..." or with, "In the words of Mark Twain...."

Proper Roasting

A roast is an event when all of the speakers insult the guest of honor.

A well-done roast is a wonderful event. The roastee, often someone who might have trouble accepting compliments, basks in a torrent of insults and gives a few back. The harshness of the insults show

how close the roaster and the roastee are. Everyone goes home having laughed themselves silly.

A badly done roast, however, can unleash an avalanche of bad feelings and plots for revenge. It is an intensely tribal event with all sorts of unwritten rules. Here are a few of them:

» The closer your relationship to the roastee, the harsher you can be. If you really know the person, you know what they can tolerate, and they know that you still love them, no matter what you are saying. It's almost an insult to go easy on your best buddy.

» The closer the group, the harsher you can be. If everyone in the room is a member of the same ethnic group, grew up in the same neighborhood, and played on the same football team, almost anything is okay.

» The exception: Don't talk about people's parents, spouse, or kids. You are only allowed to insult the roastee. It's one thing to insult me. I don't mind. If, however, you say something about my sons, I can get quite edgy.

» Tell everyone who you are. If you are the roastee's brother or former roommate from out of town, say so. That way the people in the room will know how you have the right to say all the horrible things you are about to say.

» If you are the oldest or most respectable person in the room, break the ice by letting people know that you are there to be one of the gang and that you will not take offense. Start right in saying, "For all you guys who have been leering at me, I'm Father Fallon and this is a robe, not a dress."

» Never repeat a line from a roast outside of a roast. Just say, "I laughed so hard I can't remember a thing."

» Don't bring a tape recorder of videotape recorder into a roast. This is the kind of evidence that comes back to haunt people during performance reviews at work, divorce proceedings, and political campaigns.

» When in doubt, turn the insult in on yourself, "He's no smarter than I am. We once tried to go ice fishing in July... in Philadelphia. Boy, was the rink manager peeved."

What's a Keynote?

A keynote address is the speech that is supposed to be the highlight of a meeting or conference. It's an honor to be asked to give a keynote speech, so you will want to make your speech especially memorable. Unfortunately, circumstances often make it hard to give a good keynote presentation. Many keynote presentations are scheduled during meals, so you will be competing with the clatter of dishes and the murmur of people asking each other to pass the salt.

The good news about a keynote speech is that you often get to define your own topic, instead of speaking on an assigned topic. This lets you choose the subject you care most about...unless that topic is your company's favorite product. The unwritten rule of keynotes is that you should be speaking about larger, broader issues than most of the other presenters. You are there to deliver the big picture, not to make a sale. This is hardly a hindrance for most business speakers, who can talk about their vision of the market, which, if you get deep enough into the topic, usually translates into some way in which their company is better.

If, on the other hand, you are speaking for a charity or cause, feel free to sell as hard as you want. You are here to inspire.

When you are giving a keynote, be prepared to introduce yourself and tell people why you are speaking, just in case you are not given a reasonable introduction. Tell the audience why you care about them and what experiences you have that make what you are about to say valuable to them.

Beware of the length trap. Many event organizers feel that they have to allot 45 minutes or more for a keynote. Most of the great keynote speeches we have heard, however, are shorter. If you can say what you have to say in 10 or 15 minutes, you might even be able to get the event organizers to arrange for you speak after everyone is served and before dessert, so your audience won't be busy looking for the waiters. Even if your keynote address is not scheduled during a meal, you are bound to be more fondly remembered if you deliver a message that is memorable, but short.

Being the MC

Many events have a Master of Ceremonies (MC or emcee). Once you gain a reputation of being a great speaker, the odds are that you will be asked to serve as an MC. The first thing you need to know is that, even though you have been chosen because you are a great speaker, this may not be an occasion at which you are expected to say a lot. The best MCs often stay in the background and let the other guests claim the spotlight.

When you are asked to be MC, find out just what is expected of you. They may want you to just do a few introductions. They may also be making you MC so they can invite all your friends or so they can hit you up for a big contribution.

Whatever the case, get on the phone right away and talk to the other people who will be speaking and anyone else involved.

» Learn the name of the event sponsor. Does the organization go by its full name or does it use an acronym or shortened version?

» What do they expect you to wear? Many organizations like their MCs to be dolled up in "black tie," and if you don't have that kind of outfit, the rental can be expensive.

» Pay attention to how the name of the location is pronounced. Do they say "Miz-ur –ee" or "Miz-ur-ah?" Is it "All-ban-nee" or "All-Binny?" Is it "Hew-stun" or "How-stun?"

» Make sure you know what people like to be called. Is it "Carlynn" or "Cari" or "BooBoo"?

» Confirm titles. People get promoted quickly these days, and you don't want to introduce a senior vice president as a director. Does the lady with the Ph.D. actually use the title "Doctor Tive"? Do they call the lady from the church "Sister Christen," "Reverend," or "Mother"?

» When you are introducing married women, be especially careful to find out which last name they want to use. A woman could use "Bradsell" when addressing one group, but "Rudd" when talking to another.

It's good to make a few calls so you can hear pronunciations and so you can say in your introduction, "When Hugh Miller and I were first talking about this event..." But there's nothing wrong with relying on the event coordinator to do some of the legwork for you. The coordinator should be able to give you the names and numbers of the people you want to talk to, as well as help you with things like driving directions.

Dealing With Future Speaking Invitations

Once you become known for your speaking ability, you are likely to get more and more speaking invitations. This can be great, if you have the time and the inclination.

Don't, however, fall into the trap of accepting an invitation if you are not going to have the time or energy to do things right. You never want to give the exact same speech twice. There's nothing wrong with repeating a few favorite sayings or anecdotes, but never skip the step of customizing your speech to your audience.

Part II:
Gems You
Can Use

Addiction, Substance Abuse, and Moderation

If you're asked to speak about addiction, substance abuse, and so forth, be sure you know your audience. This is not a humorous topic for some people. Definitions also vary. For some groups, coffee, chocolate, and sugar are deadly addictions. For other groups, referring to these substances as addictive could insult the harrowing struggles people have had trying to kick booze or hard drugs. When appropriate, speak about your own experience.

"Moderation in all things."
—Terrence (second century B.C.)

"The most potent thing in life is habit."
—Ovid (first century A.D.)

"When you stop drinking, you have to deal with this marvelous personality that started you drinking in the first place."
—Jimmy Breslin

"Habit is stronger than reason."
—George Santayana

"I have learned to seek my happiness by limiting my desires, rather than in attempting to satisfy them."
—John Stuart Mill

"I hate to advocate drugs, alcohol, violence, or insanity to anyone, but they've always worked for me."
—Hunter S. Thompson

"Nothing succeeds like excess."
—Oscar Wilde

"Give me chastity and self-restraint, but do not give it yet."
—St. Augustine

"You must know your limitations. I drink a bottle
of Jack Daniels a day, that's mine."
> —Lemmy Kilmister, of the heavy metal
> rock band Motorhead

"You never know what is enough unless you know
what is more than enough."
> —William Blake

Toasts

May the bloom of the face never extend to the nose.

If you drink like a fish, drink what a fish drinks.

Our drink shall be water, bright, sparkling with glee,
The gift from nature, and the drink of the free.

America

Don't make fun of America unless you know your audience very well. Some people's ideas of patriotism require them to defend the mightiest country in history against even the slightest imagined slight.

If you're saluting America and there are people from another country in the room, try to look for a way to compliment that country as a great ally, beloved neighbor, longtime friend, or ancestral home of so many of our greatest citizens.

"America is the only country deliberately founded
on a good idea."
> —John Gunther

"The youth of America is their oldest tradition."
> —Oscar Wilde

"America is God's Crucible, the great Melting Pot
where all the races of Europe are melting and
re-forming!"
> —Israel Zangwill

(Note: The "melting pot" comparison is disliked by some people who object to the idea that people who come to the United States lose their earlier identities. You may prefer to use a quote that calls the country a quilt or a bouquet.)

"America is woven of many strands.... Our fate is to become one, and yet many."
—Ralph Ellison

"[America is] not merely a nation but a nation of nations."
—Lyndon B. Johnson

"America is not like a blanket—one piece of unbroken cloth, the same color, the same texture, the same size. America is more like a quilt—many patches, many pieces, many colors, many sizes, all woven and held together by a common thread."
—Jesse Jackson

"No one flower can ever symbolize this nation. America is a bouquet."
—William Safire (regarding selection of a "national flower")

"In the field of world policy, I would dedicate this nation to the policy of the good neighbor."
—Franklin D. Roosevelt

"This is the only country that ever went to the poorhouse in an automobile."
—Will Rogers

"We must keep America whole and safe and unspoiled."
—Al Capone

"Here in America we are descended in blood and spirit from revolutionists and rebels—men and women who dared to dissent from accepted doctrine."
—Dwight D. Eisenhower

"Give me your tired, your poor,
Your huddled masses yearning to breathe free,
The wretched refuse of your teeming shore,
Send these, the homeless, tempest-tost to me:
I lift my lamp beside the golden door."
—Statue of Liberty (originally written by
Emma Lazarus in *The New Colossus*)

"America did not invent human rights. In a very
real sense...human rights invented America."
—Jimmy Carter

"America is a large, friendly dog in a very small
room. Every time it wags its tail, it knocks over a
chair."
—Arnold Toynbee

"This country will not be a good place for any of
us to live in unless we make it a good place for all
of us to live in."
—Theodore Roosevelt

"No one ever went broke underestimating the
taste of the American public."
—H. L. Mencken

"The business of America is business."
—Calvin Coolidge

"The United States has to move very fast to even
stand still."
—John F. Kennedy

Toasts

To the United States: We may have our critics, but, as the
saying goes, "immigration is the sincerest form of flattery."

To America: May we always be, as Omar Bradley said, "an
arsenal of hope."

"To her we drink, for her we pray,
Our voices silent never;
For her we'll fight, come what may,
The stars and stripes forever."
—Stephen Decatur

Animals

Talk about animals with the same respect you would use for people. If you are at an event at which an animal is celebrated, the odds are the animal is, in some way, near and dear to the people there. Listen to how your hosts talk about animals and use the same kind of language. Some people love to talk about their "pets," while certain very dedicated animal lovers don't like the word "pet" and say "animal companion."

"All I need to I know I learned from my cat."
—Suzy Becker (the title of her popular book, published in 1990)

"There are no ordinary cats."
—Sidonie Gabrielle Colette

"When I play with my cat, who knows if I am not a pastime to her more than she is to me?"
—Montaigne (Michel Eyquem de Montaigne)

"The only thing that prevents cats from killing us is that they're not big enough. But they'd love to."
—Mike Royko

"A dog teaches a boy fidelity, perseverance, and to turn around three times before lying down."
—Robert Benchley

"Happiness is a warm puppy."
—Charles M. Schultz

"A dog is the only thing on this earth that loves you more than he loves himself."
> —Josh Billings (the pen name used by 19th-century American humorist Henry Wheeler Shaw)

"It is by muteness that a dog becomes for one so utterly beyond value; with him one is at peace."
> —John Galsworthy

"To his dog, every man is Napoleon; hence the constant popularity of dogs."
> —Aldous Huxley

"Among God's creatures, two, the dog and the guitar, have taken all the sizes and all the shapes, in order not to be separated from the man."
> —Andres Segovia

"The more I see of men, the more I like dogs."
> —Madame de Stael

"Love the earth and sun and the animals."
> —Walt Whitman

"Nature teaches beasts to know their friends"
> —William Shakespeare, *Coriolanus*

Toasts

To the pets who know all our faults, and never tell a soul.

To all those we share the earth with.

To our pets: May we find friends half as faithful.

Anniversaries

When speaking at a wedding anniversary, remember that the anniversary is not about you, unless you are part of the couple. Consider keeping the spotlight on them by saying just a toast, rather than making a speech. For more material, look under Weddings (page 154). Almost anything that can be said at a wedding can be repeated on an anniversary.

> "Marriage resembles a pairs of shears, so joined that they can not be separated; often moving in opposite directions, yet always punishing anyone who comes between them."
> —Sydney Smith

> "One reason people get divorced is that they run out of gift ideas."
> —Robert Byrne

> "What ought to be done to the man who invented celebrating of anniversaries? Mere killing would be too light."
> —Mark Twain (Samuel Longhorne Clemens)

Toasts—To your spouse

To my spouse and our anniversary, which I forgot once, but will never forget again.

To my spouse:
Here's a health to the future,
A sigh for the past,
We can love and remember
And love to the last.

To my spouse:
Because I love you truly,
Because you love me, too,
My very greatest happiness
Is sharing life with you.

Toasts—To the couple

Here's to you both—A beautiful pair,
On the birthday of
Your love affair.

May your joys be as deep as the ocean
And your misfortunes as light as the foam.

May you grow old on one pillow.

May your love be as endless as your wedding rings.

Art

Unless you are an expert on art, it is better to speak about the nature of art and the courage of artists than about the specific work itself. Even if you hate the work, you can admire the courage of the individual who created it and displays it.

Note that quotes about art often seem to contradict each other. You can build a speech by using a quote you disagree with, and then countering with one that is closer to how you feel.

"Art is a jealous mistress."
—Ralph Waldo Emerson

"All day long I add up columns of figures and make everything balance. I come home. I sit down. I look at a Kandinsky and it's wonderful! It doesn't mean a damn thing!"
—Soloman Guggenheim

"We need religion for religion's sake, morality for morality's sake, art for art's sake."
—Victor Cousin

"Art for art's sake makes no more sense than gin for gin's sake."
—W. Somerset Maugham

"Art for the sake of art itself is an idle sentence.
Art for the sake of truth, for the sake of what is
beautiful and good—that is the creed I seek."
>—George Sand (Amandine Aurore Lucile
>Dupin)

"It is very good advice to believe only what an
artist does, rather that what he says about his
work."
>—David Hockney

"I like to know what a picture represents without
being told by the artist."
>—Hermione Gingold

"Black art has always existed. It just hasn't been
looked for in the right places."
>—Romare Bearden

"The greatness of art is not to find what is
common but what is unique."
>—Isaac Bashevis Singer

"Industry without art is brutality."
>—John Ruskin

"Religion and art spring from the same root and
are close kin. Economics and art are strangers."
>—Willa Cather

"All art is a revolt against man's fate."
>—André Malraux

"Art flourishes where there is a sense of adventure."
>—Alfred North Whitehead

"I shut my eyes in order to see."
>—Paul Gauguin

"Art is the most intense mode of individualism
that the world has known."
>—Oscar Wilde

"Art is the signature of civilizations."
—Jean Sibelius

"Art is interested in life at the moment when the ray of power is passing through it."
—Boris Pasternak

"In art, as in life, instinct is enough."
—Anatole France (Jacques Anatole François Thibault)

"The most beautiful thing we can experience is the mysterious. It is the source of all true art and science."
—Albert Einstein

"We must never forget that art is not a form of propaganda; it is a form of truth."
—John F. Kennedy

"Art doesn't win wars, but it's the only thing that remains after the civilizations go. Nobody knows much about the politics of certain Egyptian dynasties but people remember the art, the great things that were created."
—Robert Scull

"There is an inherent truth which must be disengaged from the outward appearance of the object to be represented. This is the only truth that matters....Exactitude is not truth."
—Henri Matisse

"The essence of all art is to have pleasure in giving pleasure."
—Mikhail Baryshnikov

"The work of art may have a moral effect, but to demand moral purpose from the artist is to make him ruin his work."
— Johann Wolfgang von Goethe

"Art imitates nature in this: not to dare is to dwindle."
>—John Updike

"Art teaches nothing, except the significance of life."
>—Henry Miller

"You use a glass mirror to see your face; you use works of art to see your soul."
>—George Bernard Shaw

"Immature artists imitate. Mature artists steal."
>—Lionel Trilling

"Art is meant to disturb."
>—Georges Braque

"Abstract Art: A product of the untalented, sold by the unprincipled to the utterly bewildered."
>—Al Capp

"Every child is an artist. The problem is how to remain an artist once he grows up."
>—Pablo Picasso

Toasts

To art: that which distinguishes man from beast.

Ben Johnson said, "Art has an enemy called ignorance." Here's to the triumph of art and the end to ignorance.

Jean Cocteau said, "Art is not a pastime but a priesthood." Here's to our priesthood.

Awards – Accepting

When accepting an award, be modest, even if you don't feel that way. The trick is to play down your accomplishments, while saying what an honor the award is, and how nice the people who are giving it to you are.

Some tactics:

› Compliment the competition. "I am especially surprised, lucky, and honored to win over such deserving competition."

› Praise the past winners.

› Say something about your team. "This award really belongs to the wonderful team of people who helped me at every step along the way. I couldn't have done it without…"

› Remember the person the award was named after.

› Talk about the organization and why their goals are important.

> "I don't deserve this. But, then again, I have arthritis, and I don't deserve that either."
> —Jack Benny

> "This is a moment I deeply wish my parents could have lived to share. My father would have enjoyed what you have generously said of me—and my mother would have believed it."
> —Lyndon B. Johnson

> "Would you let an honorary mechanic fix your brand new Mercedes?"
> —Neil Simon

> "I can live for two months on a good compliment."
> —Mark Twain (Samuel Longhorne Clemens)

> "Baloney is the unvarnished lie laid on so thick you hate it. Blarney is flattery laid on so thin you love it."
> —Bishop Fulton J. Sheen

Toasts

The only toasts you can give when accepting an award are to the people who gave you the award, to the people who helped you win it, or to your many worthy competitors who also deserve the award.

~∞~

Awards—Presenting

Presenting an award in person

This is relatively easy. Just remember that you are not the star. The person getting the award is. So keep your comments short. Don't feel you have to quote anyone. Invite the winner up and lead the audience in the applause.

This is a good time to say "we" instead of "I":

> "We are proud to present our annual award to…"

> "We could not have found a better candidate…"

> "We were delighted by [the honoree's] excellence."

Announcing an award when the winner is absent

When the winner isn't there to pick up the trophy or check, you may want to say a bit more. Here are a few good ideas:

» Read the judging criteria—"This award is given to the candidate who best exemplifies the qualities of …."

» Talk about how strong the competition was "There were so many deserving entries that it was a very difficult choice. But we chose our winner because…"

» Refer to past winners "By winning, [honoree] joins a distinguished group. Last year's winner now owns a successful Ruth's Chris Steak House franchise and a winner from a decade ago went on to join the Supreme Court…"

» Say a few things about the winner's biography. "Born in Springfield, Oregon, and a member of our organization for 10 years…"

Tip: If an award is named after someone, always devote at least one sentence to that person. Never assume that your audience remembers who that person was, what he or she did, and why the award was created.

"Let us now praise famous men, and our fathers that begat us."

—Ecclesiasticus 44:1 (from The Apocrypha)

"Only mediocrity can be trusted to be always at its best."

—Max Beerbohm

"Well done is better than well said."
—Benjamin Franklin

"Great men are meteors designed to burn so that the earth may be lighted."
—Napoleon Bonaparte

"Nothing great will ever be achieved without great men, and men are great only if they are determined to be so."
—Charles de Gaulle

"Meeting Franklin Roosevelt was like opening your first bottle of champagne; knowing him was like drinking it."
—Sir Winston Churchill

Toast

The toast for the occasion is simply: To the winner.

Babies

Before you speak about a baby, be sure to find out if the baby is a boy or a girl. If the new name is at all unusual, you may want to skip the name and just say, "this wonderful baby." For speaking purposes, all babies are beautiful and no baby should be compared to a bulldog,

Winston Churchill, or Great Aunt Edna, no matter how striking the resemblance.

See Children (page 64) for more material.

> "Out of the mouth of babes and sucklings has thou ordained strength."
> —Psalms 8:2

> "A baby is God's opinion that the world should go on."
> —Carl Sandburg

> "Infancy conforms to nobody; all conform to it."
> —Ralph Waldo Emerson

> "When I was born, I was so surprised I couldn't talk for a year and a half."
> —Gracie Allen

> "There are two things in this life for which we are never fully prepared, and that is—twins."
> —Josh Billings

> "Every baby born into the world is a finer one than the last."
> —Charles Dickens

Toasts

To babies: They will make love stronger, days shorter, nights longer, bankrolls smaller, homes happier, clothes shabbier, the past forgotten, and the future worth living for.

To babies: You've got to love them. Unfortunately, you also have to feed them and change them, too.

To the new baby, who, as the parents will soon find out, is the perfect example of minority rule.

Bachelor

Bachelor parties are dangerous territory. Any comment about how the poor dude has finally been caught and fitted with a ball and chain will doubtless get back to the bride to be or to your own spouse, fiancée, or girlfriend. The classic line, "Romance is like chess: One false move and you're mated," has landed many a person in trouble.

On the other hand, getting into a little trouble, or at least talking about it, is part of what makes a bachelor party fun. You may want to check Proper Roasting (page 31) for some additional ideas.

We have not included materials for Bachlorette parties because no one will reveal to us what really happens at one.

"All reformers are bachelors."
—George Moore

"A bachelor never quite gets over the idea that he is a thing of beauty and a boy forever."
—Helen Rowland

"Marriage is a wonderful institution, but who wants to live in an institution?"
—Groucho Marx

"A friend married is a friend lost."
—Henrik Ibsen

Toasts

May we kiss all the women we please, and please all the women we kiss.

In the immortal words of Ambrose Bierce, "Here's to woman—ah, that we could fall into her arms without falling into her hands."

May our women distrust men in general, but not us in particular.

'Tis better to have loved and lost,
Than to marry and be bossed.

To women and wine: Both are sweet poison.

Say it with flowers
Say it with eats,
Say it with kisses,
Say it with sweets,
Say it with jewelry,
Say it with drink,
But always be careful
Not to say it with ink.

Banquet

When speaking at a banquet, you will normally want to speak about the topic that interests the audience the most. But if the occasion has no other purpose than the enjoyment of good food and company, talk about the food if it's good, and about the company if the food is bad.

Never insult the food even if it looks like World War II Army surplus rations that have been coated in recycled cream sauce. Someone in the room arranged for that menu. Perhaps it reminds him or her of mother's cooking. If the organizer doesn't like the stuff, he or she is already embarrassed by how putrid it is and doesn't need you to add insult to injury.

Make it clear that you are enjoying yourself. That's what banquets are all about. The material in Drinking (page 71) will also work at banquets where everyone is drinking.

> "Strange to see how a good dinner and feasting
> reconciles everybody."
> —Samuel Pepys

> "At a dinner party one should eat wisely but not
> too well, and talk well but not too wisely."
> —W. Somerset Maugham

> "Life itself is the proper binge."
> —Julia Child

"When I write of hunger, I am really writing about love and the hunger for it, and warmth and the love of it...and it is all one."
　　　　—M.F.K. Fisher

"To eat is human, to digest, divine."
　　　　—Mark Twain (Samuel Longhorne Clemens)

"Food is an important part of a balanced diet."
　　　　—Fran Liebowitz

"An army marches on its stomach."
　　　　—Napoleon Bonaparte

"Tell me what you eat and I will tell you what you are."
　　　　—Anthelme Brillat-Savarin

"There is no love sincerer than the love of food."
　　　　—George Bernard Shaw

"He was a bold man that first ate an oyster."
　　　　—Jonathan Swift

"I'm at the age where food has taken the place of sex in my life. In fact, I've just had a mirror put over my kitchen table."
　　　　—Rodney Dangerfield

"You do not sew with a fork, and I see no reason why you should eat with knitting needles."
　　　　—Miss Piggy (regarding chopsticks)

Toasts

May we always have more occasion for the cook than for the doctor.

A full belly, a heavy purse, and a light heart.

To soup: May it be seen and not heard.

Baseball

Baseball always seems to inspire vivid writing. If you have the privilege of speaking about baseball and have any time at all, use it as an excuse to read the sports page of the newspaper, and perhaps a book or two about the sport. You'll find lots of great material. If not, use one of the gems below.

"Baseball is almost the only orderly thing in a very unorderly world. If you get three strikes, even the best lawyer in the world can't get you off."
—Bill Veeck

"Whoever wants to know the heart and mind of America had better learn baseball."
—Jacques Barzun

"[Baseball] breaks your heart. It is designed to break your heart."
—A. Bartlett Giamatti

"You're expected to be perfect the day you start, and then improve."
—Ed Vargo, Supervisor of Umpires, National League

"Baseball's very big with my people. It figures. It's the only time we can get to shake a bat at a white man without starting a riot."
—Dick Gregory

"The secret of managing is to keep the guys who hate you away from the guys who are undecided."
—Casey Stengel

"It ain't over till it's over."
—Yogi Berra

"You gotta be a man to play baseball for a living, but you gotta have a lot of little boy in you too."
—Roy Campanella

Toasts

To the only game where the defense controls the ball.

To baseball and the boys of summer.

To the game that makes people who strike out six out of 10 times heroes.

Beauty

Talking about beautiful things is easier than talking about a person's beauty. If you do compliment a person's looks, it's always a good idea to go on and praise the mind and character, too. Avoid the line "Beauty is only skin deep" unless you mean to immediately mention inner beauty, too.

The big exception: You can always rave about a bride's beauty.

"A thing of beauty is a joy forever."
—John Keats

"There is no Excellent Beauty that hath not some strangeness in the proportion."
—Francis Bacon

"I don't like standard beauty. There is no beauty without strangeness."
—Karl Lagerfeld

"When I am working on a problem, I never think about beauty...but when I have finished, if the solution is not beautiful, I know it is wrong."
—R. Buckminster Fuller

"My wife was too beautiful for words, but not for arguments."
—John Barrymore

"I always say beauty is only sin deep."
—Saki (H. H. Munro)

"I'm tired of all this nonsense about beauty being only skin deep. That's deep enough. What do you want, an adorable pancreas?"
—Jean Kerr

"Remember that the most beautiful things in the world are the most useless; peacocks and lilies, for instance."
—John Ruskin

"Ask a toad what is beauty.... He will answer that it is a female with two great round eyes coming out of her little head, a large flat mouth, a yellow belly, and a brown back."
—Voltaire (François Marie Arouet)

"Sometimes I just go [to the beauty parlor] for an estimate."
—Phyllis Diller

Toasts

To beauty: Or in the words of Charles Kingsley, "Never lose an opportunity of seeing anything beautiful. Beauty is God's handwriting."

Every day you look lovelier and lovelier—and today you look like tomorrow.

To beauty: May we never fail to see it.

Birthdays

Do not reveal, discuss, or emphasize a person's age. That's his or her job. Talk about how great the person is and how nice it is to have an occasion to pay tribute.

When in doubt, go for a toast rather than a speech. Birthdays are for celebrating.

"Growing up can take a lifetime."
—Jane Wagner

"The secret of staying young is to live honestly, eat slowly, and lie about your age."
—Lucille Ball

"I am in the prime of senility."
—Joel Chandler Harris

"The hardest years in life are those between 10 and 70."
—Helen Hayes

Toasts

To the most closely guarded secret in this country: your real age.

To Europe: where they believe that women get more attractive after 35.

May you live to be 100 years old with one extra year to repent.

Do not resist growing old—many are denied the privilege.

To old age: May it always be 10 years older than you are.

May you die in bed at age 95 shot by the jealous husband of a teenage wife.

Another candle on your cake?
Well, that's no cause to pout.
Be glad that you have strength enough
To blow the damn thing out.

Time marches on
Now tell the truth:
Where did you find
The fountain of youth?

Although another year is past
He seems no older than the last!

Bride

All comments about the bride are in the present. She has no past. This is not the time to mention her previous marriages, her escapades during spring break, or even her search for a husband.

The material in Beauty (page 56) may also be useful. When speaking about a bride, everything is beautiful. The day, the room, and especially the bride are always beautiful. However, she is never lucky. Saying she is lucky to have caught the groom or to be marrying into his fine family implies that she doesn't deserve the guy.

> "Age cannot wither her, nor custom stale her infinite variety."
> —William Shakespeare, *Antony and Cleopatra*

> "She walks in beauty, like the night of cloudless climes and starry skies; And all that's best of dark and bright meet in her aspect and her eyes."
> —Byron (George Noel Gordon, Lord Byron)

> "The hardest task in a girl's life is to prove to a man that his intentions are serious."
> —Helen Rowland

Toasts

The best toast is to say "Here's to the bride." Then sit down and let her bask in the spotlight.

Here's to the bride
And here's to the groom
And to the bride's father
Who'll pay for this room.

Here's to the prettiest, here's to the wittiest,
Here's to the truest of all who are true,
Here's to the nearest one, here's to the sweetest one,
Here's to them, all in one—here's to you.

Challenge

The best approach to adversity is to welcome it as an opportunity. The right words spoken in a moment of crisis can sometimes save the day. Look in Change (page 61) for more material.

"We become wiser by adversity; prosperity destroys our appreciation of the right."
—Seneca the Younger

"The man who is swimming against the stream knows the strength of it."
—Woodrow Wilson

"I don't say embrace trouble. That's as bad as treating it as an enemy. But I do say meet it as a friend, for you'll see a lot of it and had better be on speaking terms with it."
—Oliver Wendell Holmes Jr.

"Trouble is a part of your life, and if you don't share it, you don't give the person who loves you a chance to love you enough."
—Dinah Shore

"I believe in getting into hot water; it keeps you clean."
—G. K. Chesterton

"A woman is like a teabag; you never know how strong she is until she gets in hot water."
—Eleanor Roosevelt

"By trying we can easily learn to endure adversity. Another man's, I mean."
—Mark Twain

"You don't learn to hold your own in the world by standing on guard, but by attacking and getting well hammered yourself."
—George Bernard Shaw

"I think there is one smashing rule: Never face the facts."
>—Ruth Gordon

"There are some defeats more triumphant than victories."
>—Montaigne (Michel Eyquem de Montaigne)

"Adversity is the state in which a man most easily becomes acquainted with himself, being especially free from admirers then."
>—Samuel Johnson

Toasts

Don't let the bastards get you down.

To the School of Hardknocks: May we graduate from it someday.

To us: Because any direction we go from here is up.

Change

Change has become an important theme for speaking because so many institutions have to change to keep up with the times. You can add comments about change to almost any business speech.

"Nothing endures but change."
>—Heraclitus (fifth century B.C.)

"I have discovered in my life that there are ways of getting almost anywhere you want to go, if you really want to go."
>—Langston Hughes

"Progress is a nice word. But change is its motivator and change has its enemies."
>—Robert F. Kennedy

"...it behooves us to adapt Oneself to the Times if
one wants to enjoy Continued Good Fortune."
—Niccolo Machiavelli

"Wise and prudent men—intelligent conservatives—
have long known that in a changing world worthy
institutions can be conserved only by adjusting them
to the changing time."
—Franklin D. Roosevelt

"The oldest habit in the world for resisting change
is to complain that unless the remedy to the
disease should be universally applied it should not
be applied at all. But you must start somewhere."
—Sir Winston Churchill

"You must change in order to survive."
—Pearl Bailey

"It's hard for me to get used to these changing
times. I can remember when the air was clean and
sex was dirty."
—George Burns

Toasts

To changing: It's good for babies and it's good for us.

To change: It keeps us young and makes us old.

To change: May we always see it as an opportunity and
never as a threat.

Charity

Look at Fund-Raising (page 86) for more material.
"To err is human, to forgive, divine."
—Alexander Pope

"If you want to lift yourself up, lift up someone else."
> —Booker T. Washington

"Blessed is he who has found his work."
> —Thomas Carlyle

"Let us not paralyze our capacity for good by brooding over man's capacity for evil."
> —David Sarnoff

"Science may have found a cure for most evils; but it has found no remedy for the worst of them all—the apathy of human beings."
> —Helen Keller

"We cannot exist without mutual help. All, therefore, that need aid have a right to ask it from their fellow men, and no one who has the power of granting can refuse it without guilt."
> —Sir Walter Scott

"A good deed never goes unpunished."
> —Gore Vidal

"Understanding human needs is half the job of meeting them."
> —Adlai Stevenson

"It is with narrow-souled people as with narrow-necked bottles: The less they have in them the more noise they make in pouring it out."
> —Alexander Pope

"Everybody wants to do something to help, but nobody wants to be first."
> —Pearl Bailey

"Let us not be weary in well doing."
> —Galatians 6:9

"The desire for power in excess caused angels to fall;
the desire for knowledge in excess caused man to
fall; but in charity is no excess, neither can man or
angels come into danger by it."
—Francis Bacon

Toasts

To our benefactor: whose presents make our hearts grow
fonder.

To our benefactor: who came forward when we needed
him most, proving the old saying that "when it gets dark
enough, you will see the stars."

Children

You can make fun of children in general, but the only instance
where you can make fun of specific children is if they are your off-
spring or your students. Even then, you have to be careful. Children
who like to be teased in private may be mortified at being teased in
public.

See Babies (page 50) for additional material.

"Our children are not going to be just 'our
children'—they are going to be other people's
husbands and wives and the parents of our
grandchildren."
—Mary S. Calderone

"The child is father of the man."
—William Wordsworth

"A child develops individuality long before he
develops taste. I have seen my kid straggle into the
kitchen in the morning with outfits that need only
one accessory: an empty gin bottle."
—Erma Bombeck

"Insanity is hereditary—you get it from your children."
—Sam Levenson

"I see the mind of the 5-year-old as a volcano with two vents: destructiveness and creativeness."
—Sylvia Ashton-Warner

"Children have never been very good at listening to their elders, but they have never failed to imitate them."
—James Baldwin

"You cannot write for children....They're much too complicated. You can only write books that are of interest to them."
—Maurice Sendak

"I have found the best way to give advice to your children is to find out what they want and then advise them to do it."
—Harry S Truman

"Ask your child what he wants for dinner only if he's buying."
—Fran Liebowitz

"Mankind owes to the child the best it has to give."
—Jose Correa, U.N. Representative from Nicaragua (United Nation's Declaration of the Rights of the Child)

"The children now love luxury, they have bad manners, contempt for authority, they show disrespect for elders and love chatter in place of exercise. They no longer rise when elders enter the room. They contradict their parents, chatter before company, gobble up dainties at the table, cross their legs, and tyrannize over their teachers."
—Socrates (fifth century B.C.)

"Just as the twig is bent the tree's inclin'd."
—Alexander Pope

"I want every kid to be viewed as a person rather than as a member of a certain race."
—Michael Jordan

Toasts

To children: The future of the world.

To the innocence of children and the inner sense of adults.

As they say in the diaper business, "bottoms up."

Civil Rights

See Change (page 61) and Politics (page 118) for more material.

"I believe that unarmed truth and unconditional love will have the final word."
—Martin Luther King, Jr.

"If we cannot now end our differences, at least we can help make the world safe for diversity."
—John F. Kennedy

"There oughtn't be discrimination. Everything ought to be based on potential. Everyone should be treated alike...."
—Bob Dole

"He that complies against his will, is of his own opinion still."
—Samuel Butler

"Ask nothing that is not clearly right, and submit to nothing that is wrong."
—Andrew Jackson

"Man is born free, and everywhere he is in chains."
—Jean Jacques Rousseau

"The condition upon which God hath given liberty
to man is eternal vigilance."

> —John Philpot Curran (Irish politician and
> judge, 1790. Thomas Jefferson is often
> credited with a similar statement.)

Toasts

To America: As Carl Schurz once said, "Our country!
When right, to be kept right. When wrong, to be put right!"

To Rosa Parks and all the others who refused to step to
the rear.

Community

Communities like to hear about themselves. If you're speaking to
a geographical community, talk about its land and its history. If you're
talking about a different sort of community, talk about the common
factors that bind its members together.

See also Teamwork (page 143).

"We must turn to each other and not on each other."
—Jesse Jackson

"We must, indeed, all hang together, or most
assuredly we shall all hang separately."
—Benjamin Franklin

"We are a nation of communities, of tens ands
tens of thousands of ethnic, religious, social,
business, labor union, neighborhood, regional and
other organizations, all of them varied, voluntary
and unique."
—George Herbert Walker Bush

"When bad men combine, the good must associate."
—Edmund Burke

Toasts

To that which binds us together.

To our differences: May they always be small.

To common ground and common good.

Conventions

When speaking at a convention, your first tactic is to speak about your assigned topic or the theme of the convention. Speaking about the city you are in or about the nature of conventions is a secondary tactic for finding more material.

"A convention is a splendid place to study human nature. Man in a crowd is quite a different creature than man acting alone."
—William Jennings Bryant

"People of the same trade seldom meet together, even for merriment and diversion, but the conversation ends in a conspiracy against the public, or in some contrivance to raise prices."
—Adam Smith

"An individual starts off facing problems with a resolution to solve them—but at a convention you save the resolution for the end."
—Anonymous

Toasts

To our unconventional convention.

May we never forget those we represent.

Let us remember home while we are here, and all those we meet here when we return home.

Criticism

If you are speaking to a group of people who have been criticized, remind them that every great performer has had at least a few bad reviews.

If your purpose is to criticize, look in Protest (page 125).

If you're addressing a group of critics, say as little as possible.

> "One fifth of the people are against everything all the time."
> —Robert F. Kennedy

> "Having critics praise you is like having the hangman tell you [that] you have a pretty neck."
> —Eli Wallach

> "For the Devil mutters behind the leaves: 'It's pretty, but is it Art?'"
> —Rudyard Kipling

> "Censure is the tax a man pays to the public for being eminent."
> —Jonathan Swift

> "It is much easier to be critical than to be correct."
> —Benjamin Disraeli

Toasts

To our critics I give the words of Rudolf Bing, who said, "I am perfectly happy to believe that nobody likes us but the public."

May we learn from criticism...that our critics are wrong.

Those who can, do. Those who can't do, become critics.

Dispute

When speaking about disputes, think carefully about what you want to say. In public speaking, as in arrests, anything you say can be used against you.

"Let us never negotiate out of fear, but let us never fear to negotiate."
—John F. Kennedy

"The devil can cite Scripture for his purpose"
—William Shakespeare, *The Merchant of Venice*

"My pappy told me never to bet my bladder against a brewery or get into an argument with people who buy ink by the barrel."
—Lane Kirkland

"People are generally better persuaded by the reason which they have themselves discovered than by those which have come to the minds of others."
—Blaise Pascal

"No matter what side of an argument you're on, you always find some people on your side that you wish were on the other side."
—Jascha Heifetz

"When people are least sure, they are often most dogmatic."
—John Kenneth Galbraith

"My sad conviction is that people can only agree about what they're not really interested in."
—Bertrand Russell

"I dislike arguments of any kind. They are always vulgar, and often convincing."
—Oscar Wilde

"I respect only those who resist me, but I cannot tolerate them."
—Charles de Gaulle

"You cannot shake hands with a clenched fist."
—Indira Gandhi

Toasts

To friendship after resolution.

To our cause.

Here's to the process by which disputes drive progress.

Drinking

If you want to speak about moderation, look at Addiction, Substance Abuse, and Moderation (page 37). If you are in favor of drinking, this is the section for you. Drinking occasions are an ideal time for toasting. Toasts made early in the evening are more likely to be understood and remembered than toasts made in the wee hours.

"Tis a pity wine should be so deleterious, for tea and coffee leave us much more serious."
—Byron (George Noel Gordon, Lord Byron)

"A feast is made for laughter, and wine maketh merry."
—Ecclesiastes 10:19

"Wine nourishes, refreshes, and cheers. Wine is the foremost of medicines...wherever wine is lacking, medicines become necessary."
—The Talmud

"Give me a bowl of wine—in this I bury all unkindness."
—William Shakespeare, *Julius Caesar*

Toasts

To wine: It improves with age—the older I get, the more
I like it.

God, in His goodness, sent the grapes
To cheer both great and small;
Little fools will drink too much,
And great fools none at all.

To wine and women: May we always have a taste for both.

To women and wine: May our lips meet both.

"Then fill the cup, fill high! Fill high!
Nor spare the rosy wine,
If death be in the cup, we'll die
Such death would be divine."
                    —James Russell Lowell

Here's to the red and sparkling wine,
I'll be your sweetheart, if you'll be mine,
I'll be constant, I'll be true,
I'll leave my happy home for you.

Wine, to strengthen friendship and light the flame of love.

"God made Man,
Frail as a Bubble
God made Love
Love made Trouble
God made the vine
Was it a sin
That Man made Wine
To drown Trouble in?"
                    —Oliver Herford

To grape expectations.

Here's to a temperance supper,
With water in glasses tall,
And coffee and tea to end with—
And me not there at all.

Here's to the best key for unlocking friendship—
whis-key.

Here's to your welcome, which was cordial, and your cordial
which is welcome.

Lift 'em high and drain 'em dry
To the guy who says, "My turn to buy!"

May we never be out of spirits.

Here's to Cervantes who said, and I quote, "I drink when
I have occasion and sometimes when I have no occasion."

A glass in the hand is worth two on the shelf.

Education

See School (page 133) and Graduation (page 92) for additional
material.

"I respect faith, but doubt is what gets you an
education."
—Wilson Mizner

"Knowledge is power."
—Francis Bacon

"Education happens everywhere, and it happens
from the moment a child is born…until it dies."
—Sara Lawrence Lightfoot

"Human history becomes more and more a race
between education and catastrophe."
—H. G. Wells (1920)

"Four years was enough of Harvard. I still had a
lot to learn, but had been given the liberating
notion that now I could teach myself."
—John Updike

"Education is the ability to listen to almost anything without losing your temper or your self-confidence."
—Robert Frost

"Training is everything. The peach was once a bitter almond; cauliflower is nothing but cabbage with a college education."
—Mark Twain (Samuel Longhorne Clemens)

"Education is an ornament in prosperity and a refuge in adversity."
—Aristotle

"The gains in education are never really lost. Books may be burned and cities sacked, but truth, like the yearning for freedom, lives in the hearts of humble men."
—Franklin D. Roosevelt

"The direction in which education starts a man will determine his future in life."
—Plato

"Experience, travel—these are as education in themselves."
—Euripides

Toasts

To learning: May we never stop.

May we grow in knowledge and share what we know.

Environment

If you are talking to a group facing an environmental challenge, you may also find good material in Challenge (page 60) and Volunteerism (page 152).

"Forgive us all our trespasses, little creatures everywhere."
—James Stephens

"Accuse not nature, she hath done her part; do thou but thine."
—John Milton, *Paradise Lost*
(spoken by the archangel Raphael to Adam in the Garden of Eden)

"All art is but imitation of nature."
—Seneca (63 A.D.)

"Education is the instruction of the intellect in the laws of Nature."
—Thomas H. Huxley

"Industrialism is the systematic exploitation of wasting assets...progress is merely an acceleration in the rate of that exploitation. Such prosperity as we have known up to the present is the consequence of rapidly spending the planet's irreplaceable capital."
—Aldous Huxley

"The groves were God's first temples."
—William Cullen Bryant

"A leaf of grass is no less than the journey-work of the stars."
—Walt Whitman

"We won't have a society if we destroy the environment."
—Margaret Mead

"Hurt not the earth, neither the sea, nor the trees."
—Revelations 7:3

"Ecology is boring for the same reason that destruction is fun."
—Don DeLillo (winner of the National Book Award and the PEN/Faulkner award for fiction)

"Perhaps our age will be known to the future historians as the age of the bulldozer and the exterminator; and in many parts of the country the building of a highway has about the same result upon vegetation and human structure as the passage of a tornado or the blast of an atom bomb."
—Lewis Mumford

"The earth has a skin and that skin has diseases; one of its diseases is called man."
—Friedrich Wilhelm Nietzsche

"We must realize that we can no longer throw our wastes away because there is no 'away.'"
—William T. Cahill

"Over increasingly large areas of the United States, spring now comes unheralded by the return of the birds, and the early mornings are strangely silent where once they were filled with the beauty of bird song."
—Rachel Carson (1962)

Toasts

To mother earth.

To the balance of nature.

May we always remember that we don't own the earth. We are merely custodians.

Ethics

For additional material, see Civil Rights (page 66) and Community (page 67).

"Ask yourself not if this or that is expedient, but if it is right."
—Alan Paton

"When morality comes up against profit, it is seldom that profit loses."
—Shirley Chisholm

"For what is a man profited, if he shall gain the whole world, and lose his own soul?"
—Matthew 16:25

"I would prefer even to fail with honor than win by cheating."
—Sophocles

"No man is justified in doing evil on the grounds of expedience."
—Theodore Roosevelt

"Those who corrupt the public mind are just as evil as those who steal from the public."
—Adlai Stevenson

"Right is right, even if everyone is against it; and wrong is wrong, even if everyone is for it."
—William Penn

"I believe that unarmed truth and unconditional love will have the final word in reality. This is why right, temporarily defeated, is stronger than evil triumphant."
—Martin Luther King, Jr.

"Expedients are for the hour, but principles are for the ages."
—Rev. Henry Ward Beecher

"There is only one morality, as there is only one geometry."
> —Voltaire (François Marie Arouet)

"Indifference, to me, is the epitome of evil."
> —Elie Wiesel

"I would rather be the man who bought the Brooklyn Bridge than the man who sold it."
> —Will Rogers

Toasts

May corruption be chained, and truth maintained.

To the power of truth: In the words of Sojourner Truth, "Truth burns up error."

To truth: As it says in John 8:32, "The truth shall make you free."

Faith

Every belief system or religion has writings that provide great materials on faith. If you have time, ask a minister, a rabbi, a priest, a pundit, a monk, a chaplain, a guru, a swami, a nun, an atheist, or some other person who has thought a lot about faith for a favorite quote. The answers are often surprising.

"You can't solve many of today's problems by straight linear thinking. It takes leaps of faith to sense the connections that are not necessarily obvious."
> —Matina Horner

"I would rather live in a world where my life is surrounded by mystery than live in a world so small that my mind could comprehend it."
> —Harry Emerson Fosdick

"If there was no faith there would be no living in this world. We couldn't even eat hash with any safety."
—Josh Billings

"Not truth, but faith, it is that keeps the world alive."
—Edna St. Vincent Millay

"A casual stroll through a lunatic asylum shows that faith does not prove anything."
—Friedrich Wilhelm Nietzsche

"I believe that man will not merely endure: he will prevail. He is immortal...because he has a soul, a spirit capable of compassion and sacrifice and endurance."
—William Faulkner

"Faith may be defined briefly as an illogical belief in the occurrence of the improbable."
—H. L. Mencken

"I slowly moved into an intellectual acceptance of what my intuition had always known."
—Madeleine L'Engle

"You can do very little with faith, but you can do nothing without it."
—Samuel Butler

"Faith is much better than belief. Belief is when someone *else* does the thinking."
—R. Buckminster Fuller

"If God be for us, who can be against us?"
—Romans 8:31

Toasts

To the invisible.

To faith: May we never be without it.

Family

See also Babies (page 50), Children (page 64), Mothers (page 109), Fathers (page 83), and Parents (page 115).

"The presidency is temporary—but the family is permanent."
—Yvonne de Gaulle (wife of the French president Charles de Gaulle)

"Happiness is having a large, loving, caring, close-knit family in another city."
—George Burns

"Big sisters are the crab grass in the lawn of life."
—Charles M. Schulz

"A family is a unit composed not only of children but of men, women, an occasional animal, and the common cold."
—Ogden Nash

"All happy families are alike, but each unhappy family is unhappy in its own way."
—Leo Tolstoy

"You don't choose your family. They are God's gift to you, as you are to them."
—Desmond Tutu

"The family is one of nature's masterpieces."
—George Santayana

"To each other, we were as normal and nice as the smell of bread. We were just a family. In a family, even exaggerations make perfect sense."
—John Irving

"We are willing to spend the least amount of money to keep [an American child] at home, more to put him in a foster home, and the most to institutionalize him."
—Marian Wright Edelman

Toasts

To my sibling: Some part of every family tree has to be out on a limb.

We've toasted the mother and the daughter;
We've toasted the sweetheart and wife;
But somehow we missed her,
Our dear little sister—
The joy of another man's life.

To those who know me best and, for some reason, still love me.

May we be loved by those we love.

To the sap in our family tree.

To my cousins: Because of you, I never felt like an only child.

To our clan
The best there are
Every woman
Every man.

To the 'r' in the word brother: Without it, you'd just be a bother.

Farewell and Retirement

When you are speaking at a farewell event, be sure to monitor your feelings as you rehearse. There's nothing shameful about breaking into tears in public, but it's best to know how deeply you feel so you won't surprise yourself.

"I married him for better or worse, but not for lunch."

—Hazel Weiss, after her husband, George Weiss, retired as general manager of the New York Yankees, 1960.

"Parting is all we know of heaven, and all we need of hell."

> —Emily Dickinson

"I have made noise enough in the world already, perhaps too much, and am now getting old, and want retirement."

> —Napoleon Bonaparte

"I am convinced that the best service a retired general can perform is to turn in his tongue along with his suit and to mothball his opinions."

> —General Omar N. Bradley

"I really think it's better to retire when you still have some snap left in your garters."

> —Russell B. Long

"I'm now at the age where I've got to prove that I'm just as good as I never was."

> —Rex Harrison

"People do not retire. They are retired by others."

> —Edward "Duke" Ellington

"You can only hold your stomach in for so many years."

> —Burt Reynolds (regarding retiring briefly from films)

Toasts

May we always part with regret and meet again with pleasure.

Happy are we met, happy have we been,
Happy may we part, and happy meet again.

To your retirement: a deserved reward for a job well done.

Here's to the holidays—all 365 of them.

Fathers

See also Parents (page 115).

"It is a wise father that knows his own child."
> —William Shakespeare, *The Merchant of Venice*

"Let us now praise famous men, and our fathers that begat us."
> —Ecclesiasticus, 44:1 (from The Apocrypha)

"He may be president, but he still comes home and swipes my socks."
> —Joseph P. Kennedy

"You don't have to deserve your mother's love. You have to deserve your father's."
> —Robert Frost

Toasts

To dad: May the love and respect we express toward him make up for the worry and care we have visited upon him.

To my father: If I can become half the man he is, I'll have achieved greatness.

To the people who supply the chromosome and the reason why.

Friendship

Comments on friendship can be used for everything from close personal bonds to business alliances. Look in Community (page 67) and Teamwork (page 143) for more material. Also consider announcing that a friend is like family and using quotes from Family (page 80).

"A friend in need is a friend indeed."
—Plautus (second century B.C.)

"Happy is the house that shelters a friend!"
—Ralph Waldo Emerson

"Friendship is like money, easier made than kept."
—Samuel Butler

"One loyal friend is worth 10,000 relatives."
—Euripides

"Friendship is a single soul dwelling in two bodies."
—Aristotle

"My best friend is the one who brings out the best in me."
—Henry Ford

"We are so fond of one another because our ailments are the same."
—Jonathan Swift

"A true friend is the best possession."
—Benjamin Franklin

"I never considered a difference of opinion in politics, in religion, in philosophy, as cause for withdrawing from a friend."
—Thomas Jefferson

"The only way to have a friend is to be one."
—Ralph Waldo Emerson

"Friendship is seldom lasting but between equals, or where the superiority on one side is reduced by some equivalent advantage on the other."
—Samuel Johnson

"If I do vow a friendship, I'll perform it to the last article."
—William Shakespeare, *Othello*

"Anybody can sympathize with the sufferings
of a friend, but it requires a very fine nature to
sympathize with a friend's success."
—Oscar Wilde

Toasts

God gives us our relatives—Thank God, we can choose our friends.

May we never want a friend to cheer us, or a bottle to cheer him.

Nothing but the best for you. That's why you have us as friends.

Here's to the man who is wisest and best
Here's to the man who with judgment is blest,
Here's to the man who's as smart as can be—
I drink to the man who agrees with me!

Friendship's the wine of life.

Let's drink of it and to it.

May the friends of our youth be the companions of our old age.

May the roof above us never fall in, and may we friends gathered below never fall out.

When climbing the hill of prosperity, may we never meet a friend coming down.

To perfect friends who were once perfect strangers.

May you have more and more friends, and need them less and less.

To our friendship, which, like the wine in this glass, has mellowed and gotten better and better over time.

To our humorous friend: May you always be healthy, wealthy, and wisecracking.

Here's to those who love us well,
Those who don't can go to hell.

Here's to our absent friends: Although out of sight, we recognize them with our glasses.

May our injuries be written in sand and our friendships in marble.

Fund-Raising

If you are giving a fund-raising speech, don't be shy about it. Everyone knows why you, and they, are there. Challenge, beg, or demand—just be sure you make it clear what you want the audience to do.

Try telling this story: A pig was once complaining to a cow. The pig said, "I just don't get it. I give my meat, my hide, and even my bristles for brushes. And yet the farmer still likes you better. The cow replied, "perhaps that's because I give while I'm still alive." Your audience should get the point.

If you give a lot of fund-raising speeches to the same audience, you can surprise them by varying the story. The next time you tell it, the pig can be the more generous one because he gives his flesh, which is a greater commitment than just milk.

"Freely ye have received, freely give."
—Matthew 10:8

"Money-giving is a very good criterion...of a person's mental health. Generous people are rarely mentally ill people."
—Karl A. Menninger

"It is more blessed to give than to receive."
—Acts 20:35

"As the purse is emptied the heart is filled."
—Victor Hugo

"No one would remember the Good Samaritan
if he'd only had good intentions. He had money
as well."
—Margaret Thatcher

"Surplus wealth is a sacred trust which its
possessor is bound to administer in his lifetime
for the good of the community."
—Andrew Carnegie

"The Sea of Galilee and the Dead Sea are made of
the same water. It flows down, clear and cool, from
the heights of Hermon and the roots of the cedars
of Lebanon. The Sea of Galilee makes beauty of it,
for the Sea of Galilee has an outlet. It gets to give.
It gathers in its riches that it may pour them out
again to fertilize the Jordan plain. But the Dead
Sea with the same water makes horror. But the
Dead Sea has not outlet. It gets to keep."
—Harry Emerson Fosdick

"Money is like manure. If you spread it around,
it does a lot of good, but if you pile it up in one
place, it stinks like hell."
—Clint W. Murchison

"God loveth a cheerful giver."
—II Corinthians 9:7

"No person was ever honored for what he received.
Honor has been the reward for what he gave."
—Calvin Coolidge

Toasts

Here's to the best nation of all: donation.

To quote the good book, "God loveth a cheerful giver."
—II Corinthians 9:7

Let us remember the command, "Freely ye have received,
freely give."
—Matthew 10:8

Future

When speaking about the future, you can often focus on the idea that
the people in the room will contribute to, or even define, the future, and
then use material from Change (page 61) and Teamwork (page 143).

"Never look down to test the ground before taking your
next step; only he who keeps his eye fixed on the far
horizon will find the right road."
—Dag Hammarskjold

"Neither a wise man nor a brave man lies down
on the tracks of history to wait for the train of the
future to run over him."
—Dwight D. Eisenhower

"There is no future for a people who deny their
past."
—Adam Clayton Powell, Jr.

"These doomsday warriors look no more like
soldiers than the soldiers of the Second World
War looked like conquistadors. The more expert
they become, the more they look like lab assistants
in small colleges."
—Alistair Cooke

"We cannot always build the future for our youth,
but we can build our youth for the future."
—Franklin D. Roosevelt

"The future isn't what it used to be."
—Yogi Berra

"There is nothing like a dream to create the future."
—Victor Hugo

"Science has not yet mastered prophecy. We predict too much for the next year and yet far too little for the next 10."
—Neil A. Armstrong

"The danger of the past was that men became slaves. The danger of the future is that men may become robots."
—Erich Fromm

"I like the dreams of the future better than the history of the past."
—Thomas Jefferson

"Never let the future disturb you. You will meet it, if you have to, with the same weapons of reason which today arm you against the present."
—Marcus Aurelius Antoninus

"Only mothers can think of the future—because they give birth to it in their children."
—Maxim Gorky

"I never think of the future. It comes soon enough."
—Albert Einstein

Toasts

May Dame Fortune ever smile on you, but never her daughter, Miss Fortune.

In the words of Star Trek's Mr. Spock, "Live long and prosper."

To tomorrow.

Golf

If you are speaking during daylight hours, don't speak for too long. You may be keeping people from getting to the links.

"You drive for show but putt for dough."
—Bobby Locke

"If there is any larceny in a man, golf will bring it out."
—Paul Gallico

"If you break 100, watch your golf. If you break 80, watch your business."
—Joey Adams

"Well, they're Southern people, and if they know you are working at home, they think nothing of walking right in for coffee. But they wouldn't dream of interrupting you at golf."
—Harper Lee, on why she has done her best creative thinking while playing golf

"Give me my golf clubs, fresh air, and a beautiful partner, and you can keep my golf clubs and the fresh air."
—Jack Benny

"Golf is a good walk spoiled."
—Mark Twain (Samuel Longhorne Clemens)

Toasts

To golf: The most frustrating and masochistic sport in the world, which may be why golf spelled backwards is flog.

Here's to the golfer who just missed a hole-in-one by six strokes.

May your investments always be above par, and your game always below.

Grace

This section is about comments you make before a meal. To find material you can use on the subject of physical grace, look in Beauty (page 56). To find material you can use on the subject of religious grace, look in Faith (page 78).

When people are hungry, keep before-meal graces short. Save the rowdier graces for very informal occasions. For more possibilities, look at the toasts throughout this book. Many toasts make fine graces.

"The creator forcing man to take in food for living invites him through appetite and rewards him with pleasure."
—Anthelme Brillat-Savarin

"For what we are about to receive, may the Lord make us truly thankful."
—(Traditional)

"Some hae meat, and canna eat,
And some wad eat that want it;
But we hae meat, and we can eat,
And sae the Lord be thankit."
—Robert Burns

Toasts

In the words of the cowboys, "Bless this food and us that eats it."

Good food,
Good meat,
Good God,
Let's eat!

Rub-a-dub-dub.
Thanks for the grub.
Yeah, God!

Graduation

Graduation is one of the toughest speaking assignments. Half of the class can't wait for you to finish, and half of the class wants you to say something important and memorable. You can quote the people below, or deliver their messages in your own words.

You can also find useful material in Education (page 73) and Challenge (page 60). In fact, you can find material in almost any section, because a graduation speaker is generally allowed to speak on any topic. Feel free to make your speech about Community (page 67), Art (page 44), or Family (page 80).

> "There are no secrets to success: Don't waste time looking for them. Success is the result of perfection, hard work, learning from failure, loyalty to those for whom you work, and persistence."
> —Colin Powell

> "The fireworks begin today. Each diploma is a lighted match. Each one of you is a fuse."
> —Edward I. Koch

> "It's not at all hard for me to remember that vivid day of my own graduation. Strangely enough, the one thing about that day that I cannot remember is what the commencement speaker had to say. My thoughts, like yours, were targeted upon my family and my friends and my plans for the summer. But of one thing I'm sure: if the speaker made a short speech, I know that I blessed him."
> —Thomas J. Watson, Jr.

Toasts

A toast to the graduate—in a class by herself.

To all who have just graduated: May you now go on to become educated.

To our fine educations: May they go to our heads!

Guests and Hosts

For the most part, a toast is a more appropriate way of thanking a host or a guest than a speech.

"The guest is always right—even if we have to throw him out."
—Charles Ritz

"What is pleasanter than the tie of host and guest?"
—Aeschylus

"The ornament of a house is the friends who frequent it."
—Ralph Waldo Emerson

"Fish and visitors smell in three days."
—Benjamin Franklin

"Welcome the coming, speed the parting guest."
—Homer

Toasts

To our host, a most excellent man; for is not a man fairly judged by the company he keeps?

Here's a toast to our host from all of us;
May he soon be the guest of each of us.

Here's to our hostess, considerate and sweet;
Her wit is endless, and now let's eat.

To the sun that warmed the vineyard,
To the juice that turned to wine,
To the host that cracked the bottle,
And made it yours and mine.

In the truly immortal words of Bram Stoker's Count Dracula, "Welcome to my house. Come freely. Go safely. And leave something of the happiness you bring!"

To our guests: Our house is ever at your service.

By the bread and salt, by the water and wine,
You are welcome, friends, at this table of mine.

Health and Illness

As the population ages, we are all likely to have more and more occasions to speak about health and illness. Keep your ears open for quotable comments from relatives.

See Medicine (page 106) for more material.

"Suffering isn't ennobling, recovery is."
—Christiaan Barnard

"There are no such things as incurables, there are only things for which man has not found a cure."
—Bernard Baruch

"For extreme illnesses extreme remedies are most fitting."
—Hippocrates

"The patient, treated on the fashionable theory, sometimes gets well in spite of the medicine."
—Thomas Jefferson

"Serious illness doesn't bother me for long because I am too inhospitable a host."
—Albert Schweitzer

"Use your health, even to the point of wearing it out. That is what it is for. Spend all you have before you die."
—George Bernard Shaw

"Constant attention by a good nurse may be just as important as a major operation by a surgeon."
—Dag Hammerskjold

"Once you have been confronted with a life-and-death situation, trivia no longer matters. Your perspective grows and you live at a deeper level. There's no time for pettiness."
> —Margaretta ("Happy") Rockefeller

"The more serious the illness, the more important it is for you to fight back, mobilizing all your resources—spiritual, emotional, intellectual, physical."
> —Norman Cousins

"If you mean to keep as well as possible, the less you think about your health, the better."
> —Oliver Wendell Holmes

"Health is not a condition of matter, but of mind."
> —Mary Baker Eddy

"Look to your health; and if you have it, praise God, and value it next to a good conscience; for health is the second blessing that we mortals are capable of; a blessing that money cannot buy."
> —Izaak Walton

Toasts

Here's to your health: a long life and an easy death to you.

Here's health to all who need it.

I drink to your health when I'm with you,
I drink to your health when I'm alone,
I drink to your health so often
I'm beginning to worry about my own.

To your very good health: May you live to be as old as your jokes.

History

Talk of history as a living, breathing thing, rather than an unchanging mass. Each generation interprets the past differently, and each generation contributes to history.

Watching a program on The History Channel is another way to find material for a speech about history.

"I have but one lamp by which my feet are guided, and that is the lamp of experience. I know of no way of judging of the future but by the past."
—Patrick Henry

"The history of the world is but the biography of great men."
—Thomas Carlyle

"The history of the world is the history of a privileged few."
—Henry Miller

"History is written by the winners."
—Alex Haley

"Those who cannot remember the past are condemned to repeat it."
—George Santayana

"Legend remains victorious in spite of history."
—Sarah Bernhardt

"We are not makers of history. We are made by history."
—Martin Luther King, Jr.

"If a man could say nothing against a character but what he could prove, history could not be written."
—Samuel Johnson

"A page of history is worth a volume of logic."
—Oliver Wendell Holmes, Jr.

"Throughout history it has been the inaction of those
who could have acted, the indifference of those who
should have known better, the silence of the voice of
justice when it mattered most, that has made it
possible for evil to triumph."
—Haile Selassie

"Men and nations do behave wisely, once all other
alternatives have been exhausted."
—Abba Eban

"History is more or less bunk. It's tradition.
We don't want tradition. We want to live in
the present and the only history that is worth
a tinker's damn is the history we make today."
—Henry Ford

"We learn from history that we learn nothing from
history."
—Georg Wilhelm Friedrich Hegel

"There is a way to look at the past. Don't hide from
it. It will not catch you if you don't repeat it.'
—Pearl Bailey

"The only thing new in this world is the history
that you don't know."
—Harry S. Truman

Toasts

To the heroes of the past and the heroes of the future.

To history: Because of it, we will always have dates.

To history: May she be kind to us.

Justice

See also Civil Rights (page 66).

"A man must be willing to die for justice. Death is an inescapable reality and men die daily, but good deeds live forever."
—Jesse Jackson

"Be just before you are generous."
—Richard Brinsley Sheridan

"Ignorance of the law excuses no man."
—John Selden

"One half the world knoweth not how the other half liveth."
—François Rabelais (1532)

"Injustice is relatively easy to bear; what stings is justice."
—H. L. Mencken

"Justice is truth in action."
—Benjamin Disraeli

"Justice, sir, is the great interest of man on earth. It is the ligament which holds civilized beings and civilized nations together."
—Daniel Webster

"Delay in justice is injustice."
—Walter Savage Landor

"One man's justice is another man's injustice."
—Ralph Waldo Emerson

"Judging from the main portions of the history of the world, so far, justice is always in jeopardy."
—Walt Whitman

"Justice has nothing to do with expediency."
—Woodrow Wilson

Toasts

To vindication.

To the truth.

To doing right.

Leadership

If you are praising a leader, look at the material in Tribute (page 150).

"You do not lead by hitting people over the head—that's assault, not leadership."
—Dwight D. Eisenhower

"No man is fit to command another that cannot command himself."
—William Penn

"It's a piece of cake until you get to the top. You find you can't stop playing the game the way you have always played it."
—Richard M. Nixon

"We can't all be heroes because somebody has to sit on the curb and clap as they go by."
—Will Rogers

"A leader is a dealer in hope."
—Napoleon Bonaparte

"I never give them hell. I just tell the truth and they think it's hell."
—Harry S Truman

"Be willing to make decisions. That's the most important quality in a good leader. Don't fall victim to what I call the 'ready-aim-aim-aim-aim syndrome.' You must be willing to fire."
—T. Boone Pickens

"In time of peril, like the needle to the lodestone, obedience, irrespective of rank, generally flies to him who is best fitted to command."
—Herman Melville

"It is an interesting question how far men would retain their relative rank if they were divested of their clothes."
—Henry David Thoreau

"I will do my best. That is all I can do. I ask for your help—and God's."
—Lyndon B. Johnson,
    on arriving in Washington D.C. on the evening of John F. Kennedy's assassination, November 22, 1963

"People ask the difference between a leader and a boss.... The leader works in the open and the boss in covert. The leader leads, and the boss drives."
—Theodore Roosevelt

Toasts

Here's to our leaders who have made us winners.

Here's to leading. As they say in Alaska, only the lead sled dog has a good view.

Let's raise a glass to those who lead by example and inspiration.

Here's to leaders—appointed, elected, and otherwise selected!

Library

Also look in Education (page 73).

"I cannot live without books."
—Thomas Jefferson

"Outside of a dog, a book is the most fun you can have. Inside of a dog, it's too dark to read."
—Groucho Marx

"Literature is my Utopia. Here I am not disfranchised. No barrier of the senses shuts me out from the sweet, gracious discourse of my book friends. They talk to me without embarrassment or awkwardness."
—Helen Keller

"Reading made Don Quixote a gentleman, but believing what he read made him mad."
—George Bernard Shaw

"Until I feared I would lose it, I never loved to read. One does not love breathing."
—Harper Lee

"A man's library is a sort of harem."
—Ralph Waldo Emerson

"An art book is a museum without walls."
—André Malraux

"The chief glory of every people arises from its authors."
—Samuel Johnson

"It is with books as with men: a very small number play a great part."
—Voltaire (François Marie Arouet)

"A man loses contact with reality if he is not surrounded by his books."
—François Mitterand

> "...who kills a man kills a reasonable creature, God's image; but he who destroys a good book kills reason itself, kills the image of God, as it were, in the eye."
> —John Milton

Toasts

To books and friends: May they be few, but great.

To our library: May it speak volumes about us.

To the libraries we have slept in!

Love

Another way of finding great quotes about love is to review the lyrics of your favorite songs.

> "Love conquers all."
> —Virgil

> "The heart has its reasons, which reason does not know."
> —Blaise Pascal

> "Venus favors the bold."
> —Ovid

> "Love reckons hours for months, and days for years; and every little absence is an age."
> —John Dryden

> "It is impossible to repent of love. The sin of love does not exist."
> —Muriel Spark

> "The first duty of love is to listen."
> —Paul Tillich

"Love commingled with hate is more powerful than love. Or hate."
                              —Joyce Carol Oates

"Love cures people, the ones who receive love and the ones who give it, too."
                              —Karl A. Menninger

"Love is the only sane and satisfactory answer to the problem of human existence."
                              —Erich Fromm

"Let no one who loves be called altogether unhappy. Even love unreturned has its rainbow."
                              —James M. Barrie

"The supreme happiness of life is the conviction that we are loved."
                              —Victor Hugo

"If you want to be loved, love and be loveable."
                              —Benjamin Franklin

"It's love that makes the world go round."
                              —W. S. Gilbert

"Love like ours can never die!"
                              —Rudyard Kipling

"To fear love is to fear life, and those who fear life are already three parts dead."
                              —Bertrand Russell

"Love sought is good, but given unsought is better."
                              —William Shakespeare, *Twelfth Night*

"I am two fools, I know, for loving, and for saying so."
                              —John Donne

"One is very crazy when in love."
                              —Sigmund Freud

"The one thing that I know about love for sure is that it's the only game in town and that you must keep going back to bat again and again and again.
I have no respect for anyone who says they've given up, or that they're not looking or that they're tired. That is to abrogate one's responsibility as a human being."
—Harlan Ellison

"If love is the answer, could you rephrase the question?"
—Lily Tomlin

"Love is blynd."
—Geoffrey Chaucer

"Tis better to have loved and lost
Than never to have loved at all."
—Alfred, Lord Tennyson

"This is one of the miracles of love: it gives...a power of seeing through its own enchantments and yet not being disenchanted."
—C. S. Lewis

"It is impossible to love and be wise."
—Francis Bacon

"Love is a cunning weaver of fantasies and fables."
—Sappho

"Don't threaten me with love, baby. Let's just go walking in the rain."
—Billie Holiday

"If two people love each other, there can be no happy end to it."
—Ernest Hemingway

"I love you more than yesterday, less than tomorrow."
—Edmond Rostand

"Love is like any other luxury. You have no right
to it unless you can afford it."
　　　　　—Anthony Trollope

"Love is an exploding cigar which we willingly smoke."
　　　　　—Lynda Barry

"Love is indescribable and unconditional. I could
tell you a thousand things that it is not, but not
one that it is."
　　　　　—Edward "Duke" Ellington

"Love is like a war: easy to begin but very hard to
stop."
　　　　　—H. L. Mencken

"Love is only the dirty trick played on us to
achieve continuation of the species."
　　　　　—W. Somerset Maugham

Toasts

Here's to the happy man: "All the world loves a lover."
　　　　　—Ralph Waldo Emerson

Let's drink to love,
Which is nothing—
Unless it's divided by two.

May those now love
Who never loved before;
May those who've loved
Now love the more.

Here's to you who halves my sorrows and doubles my joys.

To the life we love with those we love.

I have known many,
Liked a few,
Loved one—
Here's to you.

Medicine

Look also at Health and Illness (page 106).

"The great secret of doctors, known only to their wives, but still hidden from the public, is that most things get better by themselves; most things, in fact, are better in the morning."
—Lewis Thomas

"Never go to a doctor whose office plants have died."
—Erma Bombeck

"The best doctor in the world is a veterinarian. He can't ask his patients what is the matter—he's got to know."
—Will Rogers

"To the person with a toothache, even if the world is tottering, there is nothing more important than a visit to a dentist."
—George Bernard Shaw

"A hospital bed is a parked taxi with the meter running."
—Groucho Marx

"Your heaviest artillery will be your will to live. Keep the big gun going."
—Norman Cousins

"God heals, and the doctor takes the fees."
—Benjamin Franklin

Toasts

Here's to those who heal.

Let us think no ill of those who help us when we are ill.

To the golden age of medicine—before HMOs.

Memorial and Funeral

See Tribute (page 150) for more material.

"When good men die, their goodness does not perish."
> —Euripedes

"It won't be long before we'll be writing together again. I just hope they have a decent piano up there."
> —Frederick Loewe (letter read at Alan Jay Lerner's memorial service)

"Whom the gods love dies young."
> —Plautus (second century B.C.)

"Every time an artist dies, part of the vision of mankind passes with him."
> —Franklin D. Roosevelt

"He was not of an age, but for all time!"
> —Ben Johnson (regarding William Shakespeare)

"Let others hail the rising sun, I bow to that whose course is run."
> —David Garrick

"If you have tears, prepare to shed them now."
> —William Shakespeare, *Julius Caesar* (Mark Anthony, speaking of Caesar)

Toasts

"Oh, here's to other meetings,
And merry greetings then,
And here's to those we've drunk with,
But never can again."
> —Stephen Decatur

To live in hearts we leave behind, is not to die.

To our dear departed, that the Devil mightn't hear of his death, 'till he's safe inside the walls of heaven.

Military

If you are speaking positively about the military, remember that people associated with the military have their own traditions and vocabulary. Make sure you have all the titles right. Do not use "mister" when talking to, or about, a captain. Also, keep your branches of the military straight. The Navy and the Coast Guard are not the same thing. Marines and Merchant Marines are not in the same organization. A sailor isn't a soldier.

People who speak negatively about the military, on the other hand, tend to ignore these distinctions and lump all of the branches together.

For more material, look in Peace (page 117).

> "The first virtue in a soldier is endurance of fatigue; courage is only the second virtue."
> —Napoleon Bonaparte

> "It is impossible to give a soldier a good education without making him a deserter. His natural foe is the government that drills him."
> —Henry David Thoreau

> "Soldiers ought more to fear their general than their enemy."
> —Montaigne (Michel Eyquem de Montaigne)

> "The military don't start wars. The politicians start wars."
> —William Westmoreland

> "Discipline is the soul of an army."
> —George Washington

"The conventional army loses if it does not win. The guerilla wins if he does not lose."
—Henry Kissinger

"No nation ever had an army large enough to guarantee it against attack in time of peace or ensure it victory in time of war."
—Calvin Coolidge

"Praise the Lord and pass the ammunition."
—Chaplain Howell M. Forgy, at Pearl Harbor

"Military intelligence is a contradiction in terms."
—Groucho Marx

Toasts

In the words of Colonel Blacker, "Put your trust in God, boys, and keep your powder dry."

Here's to the Army and Navy,
And the battles they have won,
Here's to America's colors—
The colors that never run.

Here's to the land we love and the love we land.

Mothers

See also Parents (page 115) and Children (page 64).

"I really learned it all from mothers."
—Benjamin Spock

"The hand that rocks the cradle is the hand that rules the world."
—William Ross Wallace

"My mother had a great deal of trouble with me, but I think she enjoyed it."
—Mark Twain (Samuel Longhorne Clemens)

"I looked on child-rearing not only as a work of love and duty but as a profession that was fully as interesting and challenging as any honorable profession in the world and one that demanded the best that I could bring it."
—Rose Kennedy

"You become about as exciting as your food blender. The kids come in, look you in the eye, and ask if anybody's home."
—Erma Bombeck

"Every mother is like Moses. She does not enter the promised land. She prepares a world she will not see."
—Pope Paul VI

"Men are what their mothers made them."
—Ralph Waldo Emerson

"It's like being grounded for 18 years."
—New York City Board of Education poster warning against teenage pregnancy

Toasts

To the mother who bore me,
There's no one more bold,
She's dearer by far
Than all of earth's gold.

To our father's sweethearts—our mothers.

To our mothers and all that they have meant to us. They are the proof of the Jewish proverb that "God could not be everywhere, so He made mothers."

We have toasted our sweethearts,
Our friends and our wives,
We have toasted each other
Wishing all merry lives;
Don't frown when I tell you
This toast beats all others
But drink one more toast, boys—
A toast to—our mothers.

Music and Recital

Because musicians are artists, several of the quotes listed in Art (page 44) can be used when talking about music.

"I don't sing a song unless I feel it...I have to believe in what I'm doing."
—Ray Charles

"Music hath charms to soothe a savage breast."
—William Congreve

"To produce music is also in a sense to produce children."
—Friedrich Wilhelm Nietzsche

"If I don't practice one day, I know it; two days, the critics know it; three days, the public knows it."
—Jascha Haifetz

"Nothing soothes me more after a long and maddening course of pianoforte recitals than to sit and have my teeth drilled."
—George Bernard Shaw

"Music is the universal language of mankind."
—Henry Wadsworth Longfellow

"Keep it simple, keep it sexy, keep it sad."
—Mitch Miller

"Jazz will endure as long as people hear it through their feet instead of their brains."
—John Philip Sousa

"If music could be translated into human speech, it would no longer need to exist."
—Ned Rorem

"Playing "bop" is like playing Scrabble with all the vowels missing."
—Duke Ellington

"The popular song is America's greatest ambassador."
—Sammy Cahn

"I don't know anything about music—in my line, you don't have to."
—Elvis Presley

"I can hold a note as long as the Chase Manhattan Bank."
—Ethel Merman

"Music is well said to be the speech of angels; in fact, nothing among the utterances allowed to man is felt to be so divine. It brings us near to the Infinite."
—Thomas Carlyle

"Extraordinary how potent cheap music is."
—Noel Coward

"Music is essentially useless, as life is."
—George Santayana

"It was loud in spots and less loud in other spots, and it all had that quality which I have noticed in all violin solos of seeming to last much longer than it actually did."
—P. G. Wodehouse

"Music and silence...combine strongly because music is done with silence, and silence is full of music."
> —Marcel Marceau

"Hell is full of musical amateurs."
> —George Bernard Shaw

"Music is perpetual, and only hearing is intermittent."
> —Henry David Thoreau

"If you have to ask what jazz is, you'll never know."
> —Louis Armstrong

"Music is my mistress, and she plays second fiddle to no one."
> —Edward "Duke" Ellington

"Music is either good or bad, and it's got to be learned. You got to have balance."
> —Louis Armstrong

"I have no pleasure in any man who despises music. It is no invention of ours: it is the gift of God. I place it next to theology. Satan hates music: He knows how it drives the evil spirit out of us."
> —Martin Luther

Toasts

Let's lift our glass to the conductor—a person who rarely composes himself.

Here's to those who know the score.

To harmony, and those who produce it.

Neighbors

See also Community (page 67).

"Good fences make good neighbors."
—Robert Frost

"A mystic bond of brotherhood makes all men one."
—Thomas Carlyle

"People have discovered that they can fool the devil; but they can't fool the neighbors."
—Edgar Watson Howe

"Nothing makes you more tolerant of a neighbor's party than being there."
—Franklin P. Jones

"It is easier to love humanity as a whole than to love one's neighbor."
—Eric Hoffer

"No man is an island, entire of itself; every man is a piece of the continent, a part of the main; ...any man's death diminishes me, because I am involved in mankind; and therefore never send to know for whom the bell tolls; it tolls for thee."
—John Donne

"Your own safety is at stake when your neighbor's house is burning."
—Horace

"In the field of world policy, I would dedicate this nation to the policy of the good neighbor."
—Franklin D. Roosevelt

Toasts

To the fences that separate us and the concerns that unite us.

To the views shared.

To those we borrow from.

Parents

See also Mothers (page 109) and Fathers (page 83).

"Parents have become so convinced that educators know what is best for children that they forget that they themselves are really the experts."
—Marian Wright Edelman

"You are the bows from which your children, as living arrows, are sent forth."
—Kahlil Gibran

"Here all mankind is equal: rich and poor alike, they love their children."
—Euripides

"In automobile terms, the child supplies the power but the parents have to do the steering."
—Benjamin Spock

"Parenthood remains the greatest single preserve of the amateur."
—Alvin Toffler

"If all parents today were as strict as I was, we wouldn't have so many brats and little vandals."
—Benjamin Spock's mother

"A man with parents alive is a 15-year-old boy."
—Philip Roth

"Children begin by loving their parents. After a time, they judge them. Rarely, if ever, do they forgive them."
—Oscar Wilde

"[Parents] must get across the idea that 'I love you always, but sometimes I do not love your behavior.'"
—Amy Vanderbilt

"The father is always a Republican toward his son, and his mother's always a Democrat."
—Robert Frost

"The most important thing a father can do for his children is to love their mother."
—Theodore M. Hesburgh

"People who lose their parents when young are permanently in love with them."
—Aharon Appelfeld

"Loving a child doesn't mean giving in to all his whims; to love him is to bring out the best in him, to teach him to love what is difficult."
—Nadia Boulanger

"Parentage is a very important profession, but no test of fitness for it is ever imposed in the interest of the children."
—George Bernard Shaw

"We never know the love of our parents for us until we become parents."
—Henry Ward Beecher

"The first half of our lives is ruined by our parents, and the second half by our children."
—Clarence Darrow

Toasts

To my parents, who have spoiled me my whole life long: Don't stop!

Raise a glass to those who raised us.

Here's to those who raise the citizens, and quality, of
the future.

Peace

Depending on the occasion, you might want to also consult Military (page 108), Civil Rights (page 66), or Dispute (page 70).

"The mere absence of war is not peace."
—John F. Kennedy

"People want peace so badly that governments ought
to get out of their way and let them have it."
—Dwight D. Eisenhower

"Could I have but a line, a century hence, crediting
a contribution to the cause of peace, I would yield
every honor which has been accorded by war."
—General Douglas MacArthur

"Peace is a journey of a thousand miles and it
must be taken one step at a time."
—Lyndon B. Johnson

"Nothing can bring you peace but yourself."
—Ralph Waldo Emerson

"Peace hath her victories,
No less renown'd than war."
— John Milton

"Peace, like charity, begins at home."
—Franklin D. Roosevelt

"Only a peace between equals can last."
—Woodrow Wilson

"An unjust peace is better than a just war."
—Cicero

"Peace hath higher tests of manhood
Than battle ever knew."
—John Greenleaf Whittier

"If blood be shed, let it be our blood. Cultivate the
quiet courage of dying without killing. For man
lives freely only by his readiness to die, if need be,
at the hands of his brother, never by killing him."
—Mahatma Gandhi

Toasts

May we love peace enough to fight for it.

May we love peace enough not to fight for it.

Here's to the proverbial soft answer which turneth away
wrath.

May our leaders be wise, and our commerce increase,
And may we experience the blessings of peace.

Politics

See also Voting (page 153).

"There are already far too many people in
Washington who confuse themselves with
monuments."
—Gerry Studds

"In politics stupidity is not a handicap."
—Napoleon Bonaparte

"A week is a long time in politics."
—Harold Wilson

"Politics is the art of the possible."
—Otto von Bismarck

"Politics is the art of looking for trouble, finding it everywhere, diagnosing it incorrectly, and applying the wrong remedies."
—Groucho Marx

"Politics is not the art of the possible. It consists in choosing between the disastrous and the unpalatable."
—John Kenneth Galbraith

"In politics there is no honor."
—Benjamin Disraeli

"Politics is supposed to be the second-oldest profession. I have come to realize that it bears a very close resemblance to the first."
—Ronald Reagan

"I seldom think of politics more than 18 hours a day."
—Lyndon B. Johnson

"You can't divorce religious belief and public service...and I've never detected any conflict between God's will and my political duty. If you violate one, you violate the other."
—Jimmy Carter

"Man is by nature a political animal."
—Aristotle

"Politics are almost as exciting as war and quite as dangerous. In war you can only be killed once, but in politics many times."
—Sir Winston Churchill

"Being a president is like riding a tiger...keep on riding or be swallowed. A president is either constantly on top of events or...events will soon be on top of him."
—Harry S Truman

"Politics is like being a football coach. You have to be smart enough to understand the game, and stupid enough to think it's important."
—Eugene McCarthy

"Politics is perhaps the only profession for which no preparation is thought necessary."
—Robert Louis Stevenson

"The most successful politician is he who says what everybody is thinking most often and in the loudest voice."
—Theodore Roosevelt

"An independent is the guy who wants to take the politics out of politics."
—Adlai Stevenson

"A radical is a man with both feet firmly planted in the air."
—Franklin D. Roosevelt

"The middle of the road is all of the usable surface. The extremes, right and left, are in the gutters."
—Dwight D. Eisenhower

"Doublethink means the power of holding two contradictory beliefs in one's mind simultaneously, and accepting both of them."
—George Orwell

"Ideas are great arrows, but there has to be a bow. And politics is the bow of idealism."
—Bill Moyers

"Politicans are the same all over. They promise to build a bridge even when there's no river."
—Nikita Kruschev

"The first requirement of a statesman is that he be dull. This is not always easy to achieve."
—Dean Acheson

"Ninety-eight percent of the adults in this country
are decent, hard-working Americans. It's the
other lousy two percent that get all the publicity.
But then—we elected them."
> —Lily Tomlin

"A politician is an animal that can sit on a fence and
keep both ears to the ground."
> —H. L. Mencken

"I won't eat anything that has intelligent life, but
I would gladly eat a network executive or a
politician."
> —Marty Feldman

"What is the use of being elected or re-elected
unless you stand for something?"
> —Grover Cleveland

"When I was a boy, I was told that anybody could
become president; I'm beginning to believe it."
> —Clarence Darrow

"Frankly, I don't mind not being president. I just
mind that somebody else is."
> —Edward M. Kennedy

"I like to operate like a submarine on sonar.
When I am picking up noise from both the left
and the right, I know my course is correct."
> —Gustavo Díaz Ordaz, while campaigning for
> the presidency of Mexico

"The short memories of American voters is what
keeps our politicians in office."
> —Will Rogers

"I am not a perfect servant. I am a public servant
doing my best against the odds. As I develop and
serve, be patient. God is not finished with me yet."
> —Jesse Jackson

"Since a politician never believes what he says, he is surprised when others believe him."
—Charles de Gaulle

"Mothers all want their sons to grow up to be President, but they don't want them to become politicians in the process."
—John F. Kennedy

"You campaign in poetry. You govern in prose."
—Mario Cuomo

"Every man who takes office in Washington either grows or swells, and when I give a man an office, I watch him carefully to see whether he is swelling or growing."
—Woodrow Wilson

"Some members of the Congress are the best actors in the world."
—Shirley Chisholm

"If nominated, I will not accept; if elected, I will not serve."
—General William T. Sherman

"If it walks like a duck, and quacks like a duck, then it just may be a duck."
—Walter Reuther, trade union leader, on how to tell a Communist

"You really have to get to know Dewey to dislike him."
—Robert A. Taft

Toasts

Give us pure candidates and a pure ballot-box,
And our freedom shall stand as firm as the rocks.

To Washington, our country's capital, where the roads, and everything else, go around in circles.

To the politician: a person who divides his time between running for office and running for cover.

Here's to our politician: a man who stands for what he thinks others will fall for.

To our flag, long may it wave;
And to our politicians, long may they rave!

Pride

See also History (page 96) and Faith (page 78).

"You are a very special person—become what you are."
—Desmond M. Tutu

"One of the greatest diseases is to be nobody to anybody."
—Mother Teresa

"No one can make you inferior without your consent."
—Eleanor Roosevelt

"It is better to be hated for what one is than loved for what one isn't."
—André Gide

"We need to haunt the halls of history and listen anew to the ancestors' wisdom."
—Maya Angelou

Toasts

To our daring. As they say, "No guts, no glory."

Here's to great ambition,
About which people rant.
It makes you want to do the things
That everyone knows you can't.

Good, better, best;
Never let it rest,
Till your good is better,
And your better best.

Prosperity

Check Sales (page 132) for more material.

"Seek wealth, it's good."
—Ivan Boesky

"The first rule [of becoming wealthy] is not to
lose money. The second rule is not to forget the
first rule."
—Warren Buffet

"The millionaire [has] become common in
numbers, common in the source of wealth,
common (in the usage of bygone snobberies)
in social origin, common in the continued
narrowing of the gap between his fortune and
that of the normally affluent middle class."
—Robert Heller

"To turn $100 into $110 is work. To turn $100
million into $110 million is inevitable."
—Edgar Bronfman

"If you can count your money, you don't have
a billion dollars."
—J. Paul Getty

"Affluence means influence."
—Jack London

"I have been poor and I have been rich. Rich
is better."
—Sophie Tucker

"It is better to live rich than die rich."
 —Samuel Johnson

"To be thought rich is as good as to be rich."
 —William Makepeace Thackeray

"A man is rich in proportion to the number of things he can afford to let alone."
 —Henry David Thoreau

"No man actually owns a fortune. It owns him."
 —A. P. Giannini

"The rich are different."
 —F. Scott Fitzgerald

"The rich are different—they have more money."
 —Ernest Hemingway, in response to Fitzgerald

Toasts

Here's to beauty, wit, and wine and to a full stomach, a full purse, and a light heart.

To prosperity: May each of us always keep the "me " in "economy."

May your shadow never grow less.

Protest

Look in Change (page 61), Civil Rights (page 66), and Criticism (page 69) for more material.

"Truth never damages a cause that is just."
 —Mahatma Gandhi

"Moderation in the pursuit of justice is no virtue."
 —Barry H. Goldwater

"That only a few, under any circumstances,
protest against the injustice of long-established
laws and customs, does not disprove the fact of
the oppressions, and while the satisfaction of the
many, if real, only proves their apathy and deeper
degradation."
—Elizabeth Cady Stanton

"All human things are subject to decay
And, when Fate summons, Monarchs must obey."
—John Dryden

"Be always sure you're right—then go ahead!"
—David Crockett's motto

Toasts

To the spirit of the Boston Tea Party.

To truth, not power.

To history: She will vindicate us.

Reunions

The material here is mainly oriented toward school reunions. If you are speaking at a family reunion, check the Family (page 80) for material.

"[We look like] a road company of the Last Supper."
—Dorothy Parker, on her fellow
companions at the celebrated
Algonquin Round Table

"We never had a 10th-year reunion, which was just
as well with me. The principal's office statute of
limitations probably doesn't run out in 10 years. They
might have had something on me."
—Lewis Grizzard

"Benjamin Franklin said, 'Fish and visitors smell in three days,' but old friends from college usually smell already."
—P. J. O'Rourke

"You can't go home again."
—Thomas Wolfe

"Forsake not an old friend; for the new is not comparable to him: A new friend is as new wine when it is not old, thou shalt not drink it with pleasure."
—Ecclesiasticus, 9:10 (from The Apocrypha)

Toasts

Here's a toast to all who are here,
No matter where you're from;
May the best day you have ever seen
Be worse than the worst to come.

To the good old days—which we are having right now.

In the immortal words of William Makepeace Thackeray,
"I drink it as the Fates ordain it,
Come, fill it, and have done with rhymes;
Fill up the lonely glass, and drain it
In memory of dear old times."

To our absent friends: Although they are out of sight, we recognize them with our glasses.

To the good old days—when we weren't so good, because we weren't so old.

Here's to us that are here, to you that are there, and the rest of us everywhere.

To friends—as long as we are able
To lift our glasses from the table.

"But fill me with the old familiar juice,
Methinks I might recover bye and bye."
— Omar Khayyám

Hail, hail, the gang's all here,
So what the hell do we care?
What the hell do we care?
Hail, hail, the gang's all here,
So what the hell do we care now?

Roast–Giving

Consult Proper Roasting (page 31) for tips about Roasts.

"He's about as straight as the Yellow Brick Road."
— Mart Crowley

"I'm fond of Steve Allen, but not as much as he is."
— Jack Paar, about Steve Allen

"The female of the species is more deadly than
the male."
— Rudyard Kipling

"He who allows himself to be insulted deserves to be."
— Pierre Corneille

"He has much to be modest about."
— Sir Winston Churchill, about Clement
Atlee

Anonymous Insults

There's no way this roast will make an ass out of
him—nature did that long ago.

In my book she's a great lady; but my book is
fiction.

There are many things you could say about her.
That she's modest, kind, bright, and polite. They'd
all be lies; but you could say them.

It's appropriate that we give her a dinner;
everyone does. She hasn't picked up a check in
years.

We thought it would be good to get together and say
nice things about her—but then we decided to tell
the truth, so we are having this roast.

They wanted to have him roasted by a close friend—
but they couldn't find one, so I came instead.

I'm proud to be here to honor her. I love her. I
have no taste, but I love her.

We wanted to give her something she really needs,
but we couldn't figure out how to wrap a bathtub.

A lot of nice things have been said about you
tonight: Your friends are either very dumb or very
good liars.

What can you say about our guest of honor that
hasn't been said about hazardous waste?

I'm not sure why we decided to give him such a
great going-away gift: maybe to let him know how
much we appreciate all he's done; maybe to keep
him quiet.

We wanted to give him a piece of the office. We
clearly can't give him the elevator, but we can
always give him the shaft.

His wife is delighted that he's here today. While
he's away she's having his cage cleaned.

You've got to give the woman credit. She's the only one
I know who's dumb enough to come to this little
gathering with an open mind, a complete lack of
prejudice, and a cool willingness to hear the rubbish
we're about to dump on her.

The chairman would have been here, except for the
distance: He's in the lobby.

I can only give our friend here one piece of advice.
and it comes from that great American
philosopher W.C. Fields. "If at first you don't
succeed, try, try again. Then give up. No use being
a damn fool about it."

Roast—Being the Target

If your friends decide to roast, fire back with as much ammunition as you can find. If the roast is a symbol of affection, you'll be
showing them how much you love them back. If the roast is not meant
as a token of their respect for you, hitting back will make them think
twice before tangling with you again.

If you prefer, you can use Cyrano's tactic and insult yourself more
eloquently and completely than they have the wits to do.

So you're going to try and roast me. Well, as Pat
Benatar says in her song, "Hit me with your best
shot."

I came to this event knowing that you would seek
to injure me with your wordplay, but I am not
afraid. Why? Because I'm protected by a mantra
that was passed on to me by my wise ancestors. It
goes like this: "Stick and stones may break my
bones, but names will never hurt me. Nay-nay-a-
boo-boo."

If you are going to roast me, keep it fair. Don't, for example, make a big thing about the fact that I go out with younger women. I have to. As George Burns said, "All the women my age are dead."

To all those who wish to roast me, I have just one piece of advice. Remember that when you point a finger, three fingers are pointing back at you.

Before you make your comments too biting, remember I'm the vengeful type. How much rest do you think you'll get sleeping with one eye open?

I'll admit I'm from a small town. You know how the big cities have professional call girls? In our little town, we had to make do with volunteers.

Before you begin to roast me, think of what I know about you. Think of the *years* we've worked together. I know where the bodies are buried.

I take the fact that you are going to roast me as a sign of my success and your incredible jealousy. Ambrose Bierce said it best when he defined success as "the one unpardonable sin against one's fellows."

I thought I was going to be roasted! You people don't have enough fire power to roast a peanut!

Talk about me, but not about my family: I belong to the Fred Allen school of ancestry and its motto is "I don't want to look up my family tree because I know I'm the sap."

When I look at this fine collection of friends gathered here to insult me, I can only think of Julius Caesar's last words: "Et tu, Brute?"

When you told me you were going to roast me I
thought, "Naturally, they only crucify the innocent."

So, I am to be roasted. I guess that's what happens
to a big ham.

Sales

If you are speaking to people in sales, be direct. If you manage
them, tell them what you want them to do, and how it will make them
richer.

"Blessed is he who expects nothing, for he shall
never be disappointed."
—Alexander Pope

"If you don't sell, it's not the product that's wrong,
it's *you*."
—Esteé Lauder

"There is no such thing as 'hard sell' and 'soft sell.'
There is only 'smart sell' and "stupid sell.'"
—Leo Burnett

"Everyone lives by selling something."
—Robert Louis Stevenson

"People will buy anything that's one to a customer."
—Sinclair Lewis

"Any fool can paint a picture, but it takes a wise
man to be able to sell it."
—Samuel Butler

"There's a sucker born every minute."
—P. T. Barnum

"There are no dumb customers."
—Peter Drucker

Toasts

Here's to the pressure we face—for it is, after all, pressure that turns coal into diamonds.

Here's to us: Never sell a salesperson short.

Here's to opening accounts and closing deals!

School

See also Education (page 73).

"There is only one good—knowledge; and only one evil—ignorance."
—Socrates

"You send your child to the schoolmaster, but 'tis the schoolboys who educate him."
—Ralph Waldo Emerson

"For every one of us that succeeds, it's because there's somebody there to show you the way out. The light doesn't necessarily have to be in your family; for me it was teachers and school."
—Oprah Winfrey

"I read Shakespeare and the Bible, and I can shoot dice. That's what I call a liberal education."
—Tallulah Bankhead

"A nation that continues to produce soft-minded men purchases its own spiritual death on the installment plan."
—Martin Luther King, Jr.

"In old days men studied for the sake of self-improvement; nowadays men study in order to impress other people."
—Confucius (fifth century B.C.)

"We cannot always build the future for our youth, but we can build our youth for the future."
—Franklin D. Roosevelt

"I consider a human soul without education like marble in a quarry, which shows none of its inherent beauties until the skill of the polisher sketches out the colors, makes the surface shine, and discovers every ornamental cloud, spot, and vein that runs through it."
—Joseph Addison

"To the strongest and quickest mind it is far easier to learn than to invent."
—Samuel Johnson

"It is important that students bring a certain ragamuffin, barefoot irreverence to their studies; they are not here to worship what is known, but to question it."
—Jacob Bronowski

"It is always the season for the old to learn."
—Aeschylus

"Only the educated are free."
—Epicetus (first century B.C.)

"Education is a method by which one acquires a higher grade of prejudice."
—Laurence J. Peter

"What we want is to see the child in pursuit of knowledge, and not knowledge in pursuit of the child."
—George Bernard Shaw

"Sixty years ago I knew everything; now I know nothing; education is a progressive discovery of our own ignorance."
—Will Durant

"Much learning does not teach understanding."
—Heraclitus

"It is one thing to show a man that he is in error, and another to put him in possession of truth."
—John Locke

"Just as eating against one's will is injurious to health, so study without a liking for it spoils the memory, and it retains nothing it takes in."
—Leonardo da Vinci

"You can get help from teachers, but you are going to have to learn a lot by yourself, sitting alone in a room."
—Theodore Geisel ("Dr. Seuss")

"Learn as though you would never be able to master it; hold it as though you would be in fear of losing it."
—Confucius

"Education is helping the child realize his potentialities."
—Erich Fromm

"A man who has never gone to school may steal from a freight car; but if he has a university education, he may steal the whole railroad."
—Theodore Roosevelt

"Do you know the difference between education and experience? Education is when you read the fine print; experience is what you get when you don't."
—Pete Seeger

"Against human nature one cannot legislate. One can only try to educate it, and it is a slow process with only a distant hope of success."
—Bernard Berenson

"The common school, improved and energized as it can easily be, may become the most effective and benignant of all the forces of civilization."
　　　—Horace Mann

"I am convinced that it is of primordial importance to learn more every year than the year before. After all, what is education but a process by which a person begins to learn how to learn."
　　　—Peter Ustinov

"America is the only country left where we teach languages so that no pupil can speak them."
　　　—Alfred Kazin

"Education is what survives when what has been learnt has been forgotten."
　　　—B. F. Skinner

"The test and the use of man's education is that he finds pleasure in the exercise of his mind."
　　　—Jacques Barzun

"It is no matter what you teach them first, any more than what leg you shall put into your breeches first. You may stand disputing which is best to put in first, but in the mean time your breech is bare. Sir, while you are considering which of two things you should teach your child first, another boy has learnt them both."
　　　　　　—Samuel Johnson, replying to the question of what should be the first lesson taught to children.

"You can't expect a boy to be vicious until he's been to a good school."
　　　—Saki (H. H. Munro)

"Show me the man who has enjoyed his school days and I will show you a bully and a bore."
　　　—Robert Morley

"I don't want to send them to jail. I want to send them to school."

> —Adlai Stevenson, U.S. representative to the United Nations, on picketers who attacked him in Dallas

"A child must feel the flush of victory and the heart-sinking of disappointment before he takes with a will to the tasks distasteful to him and resolves to dance his way through a dull routine of textbooks."

> —Helen Keller

"The world's great men have not commonly been great scholars, nor great scholars great men."

> —Oliver Wendell Holmes

"I believe that the school is primarily a social institution. Education being a social process, the school is simply that form of community life in which all those agencies are concentrated that will be most effective in bringing the child to share in the inherited resources of the race, and to use his own powers for social ends."

> —John Dewey

"In real life, I assure you, there is no such thing as algebra."

> —Fran Liebowitz

"A professor must have a theory as a dog must have fleas."

> —H. L. Mencken

"The city is the teacher of the man."

> —Simonides (fifth century B.C.)

"What nobler employment, or more valuable to the state, than that of the man who instructs the rising generation?"

> —Cicero

"This instrument [radio] can teach. It can illuminate,
yes, and it can even inspire. But it
can do so only to the extent that humans are
determined to use it to those ends. Otherwise
it's nothing but wires and lights in a box."
> —Edward R. Murrow

"A university should be a place of light, of liberty,
and of learning."
> —Benjamin Disraeli

"Learning is its own exceeding great reward."
> —William Hazlitt

"The idea of a college education for all young
people of capacity, provided at nominal cost by
their own states, is very peculiarly American.
We in America invented the idea. We in America
have developed it with remarkable speed."
> —Lyndon B. Johnson

"We expect teachers to handle teenage pregnancy,
substance abuse, and the failings of the family. Then
we expect then to educate our children."
> —John Sculley

"Teaching is not a lost art, but regard for it is a
lost tradition."
> —Jacques Barzun

"The use of a university is to make young
gentlemen as unlike their fathers as possible."
> —Woodrow Wilson

Toasts

To the professor: a man who talks in his students' sleep.

To our teacher: a person whose job it was to tell us how to
solve the problems of life, which he himself had avoided by
becoming a professor.

To our teacher:
Addition to your friends,
Subtraction from wants,
Multiplication of your blessings,
Division among your foes.

Science

See also Future (page 88).

"Man is slightly nearer to the atom than to the star.
From his central position man can survey the
grandest works of Nature with the astronomer, or
the minutest works with the physicist."
—Arthur Stanley

"The scientific theory I like best is that the rings of
Saturn are composed entirely of lost airline luggage."
—Mark Russell

"Is ditchwater dull? Naturalists with microscopes
have told me that it teems with quiet fun."
—G. K. Chesterton

"Every great advance in science has issued from a
new audacity of imagination."
—John Dewey

"Freedom is absolutely necessary for the progress
in science and the liberal arts."
—Benedict Spinoza

"Every great advance in natural knowledge has
involved the absolute rejection of authority."
—Aldous Huxley

"Science is the great antidote to the poison of
enthusiasm and superstition."
—Adam Smith

"When a man sits with a pretty girl for an hour, it seems like a minute. But let him sit on a hot stove for a minute—and it's longer than any hour. That's relativity."

—Albert Einstein

"Mathematics is the only science where one never knows what one is talking about nor whether what is said is true."

—Bertrand Russell

"[Scientists are] peeping Toms at the keyhole of eternity."

—Arthur Koestler

"I cannot conceive of any condition which would cause this ship to founder. I cannot conceive of any vital disaster happening to this vessel. Modern shipbuilding has gone beyond that."

—E. J. Smith, captain of the Titanic

"Science is the record of dead religions."

—Oscar Wilde

"Science can not only make man richer—but science can make man better."

—Lyndon B. Johnson

"Men love to wonder, and that is the seed of our science."

—Ralph Waldo Emerson

"Man is an animal with primary instincts of survival. Consequently, his ingenuity has developed first and his soul afterwards. Thus the progress of science is far ahead of man's ethical behavior."

—Charlie Chaplin

"The whole of science is nothing more than a refinement of everyday thinking."

—Albert Einstein

"We must, however, acknowledge, as it seems to me, that man with all his noble qualities...still bears in his bodily frame the indelible stamp of his lowly origin."
—Charles Darwin

Toasts

To Newton, and the gravity of scientific thought.

To the triumph of knowledge over superstition.

My hypothesis is that this wine is good for us. Let's test it.

Sports

For additional material see Baseball (page 55), Golf (page 90), and Tennis (page 144).

"Show me a good loser in professional sports and I'll show you an idiot."
—Leo Durocher

"I do not in the least object to a sport because it is rough."
—Theodore Roosevelt

"Serious sport has nothing to do with fair play. It is bound up with hatred, jealousy, boastfulness, disregard of all rules and sadistic pleasure in witnessing violence: in other words it is war minus the shooting."
—George Orwell

"Generally speaking, I look upon [sports] as dangerous and tiring activities performed by people with whom I share nothing except the right to trial by jury."
—Fran Liebowitz

"Winning isn't everything. It's the only thing."
—Vince Lombardi

"Competition in play teaches the love of the free spirit to excel by its own merit. A nation that has not forgotten how to play, a nation that fosters athletics, is a nation that is always holding up the high ideal of equal opportunity for all. Go back through history and find the nations that did not play and had no outdoor sports, and you will find the nations of oppressed peoples."
—Warren G. Harding

Toasts

Here's to the man who made us winners.

Here's to our coach: a man who's willing to lay down our lives for his school.

To the folks for whom sweat is sweet.

Let's drink to the coach—and hope he doesn't catch us!

To those whose bodies are temples: May you never build an unwanted addition.

To the profound ignorance which we brought to this endeavor; because had we known what was ahead, we never would have started.

Here's to the sweet smell of success.

Here's to General Douglas MacArthur who said, "There is no substitute for victory."

Let's have a drink,
Let's have some fun
Because at last
The job is done.

Teamwork

See also Community (page 67).

"We must, indeed, all hang together, or most
assuredly we shall all hang separately."
—Benjamin Franklin

"I hand him a lyric and get out of his way."
—Oscar Hammerstein, on partnership
with Richard Rogers

"A song without music is a lot like H2 without the O."
—Ira Gershwin

"When bad men combine, the good must
associate; else they will fall, one by one, an
unpitied sacrifice in a contemptible struggle."
—Edmund Burke

"All for one, one for all."
—Alexandre Dumas, the Elder
(the motto of the Musketeers)

"Never doubt that a small group of thoughtful,
committed citizens can change the world. Indeed,
it's the only thing that ever has."
—Margaret Mead

"I never could understand how two men can write
a book together; to me that's like three people
getting together to have a baby."
—Evelyn Waugh

Toasts

To what we can do together.

To the team: We will always be in our own league!

Tennis

Depending on the occasion, you may be able to spice up your speech with wordplay around the terms love and service.

"The serve was invented so that the net can play."
—Bill Cosby

"People don't seem to understand that it's a damn war out there."
—Jimmy Connors

"Tennis is a perfect combination of violent action taking place in an atmosphere of total tranquility."
—Billie Jean King

"When we have match'd our racquets to these balls,
We will, in France, by God's grace play a set
Shall strike his father's crown into the hazard."
—William Shakespeare, *Henry V*

"My advice to young players is to see as much good tennis as possible and then attempt to copy the outstanding strokes of the former stars."
—Bill Tilden

"This taught me a lesson, but I'm not sure what it is."
—John McEnroe, on losing a tournament

Toasts

To tennis: May we all have net gains.

To tennis: the only excuse that some women get for wearing white.

Here's to those who have the guts to be in the tennis racket.

Here's to tennis: the sport where love means nothing.

Theater

You may also be able to use some of the material in Music and Recital (page 111), Art (page 44), and Criticism (page 69).

"The theater is so endlessly fascinating because it's so accidental. It's so much like life."
—Arthur Miller

"Consider the public....Never fear it nor despise it. Charm it, interest it, stimulate it, shock it now and then if you must, make it laugh, make it cry, but above all...never, never bore the living hell out of it."
—Noel Coward

"The play's the thing
 Wherein I'll catch the conscience of the king."
—William Shakespeare, *Hamlet*

"It is extremely difficult thing to put on the stage anything which runs contrary to the opinions of a large body of people."
—George Bernard Shaw

"If you really want to help the American theater, don't be an actress, dahling. Be an audience."
—Tallulah Bankhead

"Whoever condemns the theater is an enemy of his country."
—Voltaire (François Marie Arouet)

"I got all the schooling any actress needs. That is, I learned to write well enough to sign contracts."
—Hermione Gingold

"All the world's a stage,
And all the men and women merely players:
They have their exits and their entrances;
And one man in his time plays many parts."
—William Shakespeare, *As You Like It*

"Comedians on the stage are invariably suicidal
when they get home."
—Elsa Lanchester

"On the stage he was natural, simple, affecting;
'Twas only that when he was off he was acting."
—Oliver Goldsmith

"Acting is merely the art of keeping a large group
of people from coughing."
—Ralph Richardson

"Know your lines and don't bump into the furniture."
—Spencer Tracy

"After my screen test, the director clapped his
hands gleefully and yelled, 'She can't talk! She
can't act! She's sensational!'"
—Ava Gardner

"Acting is all about honesty. If you can fake that,
you've got it made."
—George Burns

"Lead the audience by the nose to the thought."
—Laurence Olivier

"Your motivation is your pay packet on Friday.
Now get on with it."
—Noel Coward

"Acting is standing up naked and turning around
slowly."
—Rosalind Russell

"Some of the greatest love affairs I've known
involved one actor, unassisted."
—Wilson Mizner

"Anyone who works is a fool. I don't work—I
merely inflict myself on the public."
—Robert Morley

Toasts

Break a leg!

To our never outgrowing our current stage.

To our lines: May they never be cut.

Tragedy and Misfortune

For additional material see Challenge (page 60) and Memorial and Funeral (page 107).

"Into each life some rain must fall."
—Henry Wadsworth Longfellow

"We become wiser by adversity; prosperity destroys our appreciation of the right."
—Seneca the Younger

"Trouble is a part of your life, and if you don't share it, you don't give the person who loves you a chance to love you enough."
—Dinah Shore

"If we had no winter, the spring would not be so pleasant; if we had not sometimes taste of adversity, prosperity would not be so welcome."
—Anne Bradstreet

"Our energy is in proportion to the resistance it meets."
—William Hazlitt

"The greater the difficulty, the greater the glory."
—Cicero

"Can anybody remember when the times were not hard and money not scarce?"
—Ralph Waldo Emerson

Toasts

To better times.

To the dawn, which surely will follow this darkest hour.

Here's to you, my honest friend,
Wishing these hard times to mend.

To the difficulties that we have encountered, in acknowledgement of the fact that they have made us stronger.

Travel

You may find more material in Change (page 61).

"Unusual travel suggestions are dancing lessons from the gods."
—Kurt Vonnegut

"He hears a different drummer. Let him step to the music which he hears."
—Henry David Thoreau

"He travels fastest who travels alone."
—Rudyard Kipling

"Travel teaches toleration."
—Benjamin Disraeli

"They spell it Vinci and pronounce it Vinchy; foreigners always spell better than they pronounce."
—Mark Twain (Samuel Longhorne Clemens)

"There are two classes of travel—first class, and with children."
—Robert Benchley

"It is amazing how nice people are to you when they know you are going away."
—Michael Arlen

"He who would travel happily must travel light."
—Antoine de Saint-Exupéry

"Experience, travel—these are as education in themselves."
—Euripides

"Restore human legs as a means of travel. Pedestrians rely on food for fuel and need no special parking facilities."
—Lewis Mumford

"There is nothing so good for the human soul as the discovery that there are ancient and flourishing civilized societies which have somehow managed to exist for many centuries and are still in being though they have had no help from the traveler in solving their problems."
—Walter Lippmann

"Journeys, like artists, are born and not made. A thousand differing circumstances contribute to them, few of them willed or determined by the will—whatever we may think."
—Lawrence Durrell

"Everybody wants to be someplace he ain't. As soon as he gets there, he wants to go right back."
—Henry Ford, on why he went into the car business

"I shall always be glad to have seen it—for the same reason Papa gave for being glad to have seen Lisbon—namely 'that it will be unnecessary ever to see it again.'"
—Sir Winston Churchill, on Calcutta

Toasts

As Kermit the Frog said, "Wherever you go, there you are."

Here's to you and here's to me,
Wherever we may roam;
And here's to the health and happiness
Of the ones who are left at home.

"A health to the man on the trail tonight;
may his grub hold out; may his dogs keep their legs;
may his matches never misfire."
—Jack London

May the road rise to meet you. May the wind be always at your back, the sun shine warm upon your face, the rain fall soft upon your fields, and until we meet again may God hold you in the hollow of His hand.

Tribute

See also Awards—Presenting (page 49).

"His life was gentle and the elements so mixed in him that nature might stand on its feet and say to all the world—this was a man!"
—William Shakespeare, *Julius Caesar*

"Nothing grows well in the shade of a big tree."
—Constantin Brancusi

"No great man ever complains of want of opportunity."
—Ralph Waldo Emerson

"To be a great champion you must believe you are the best. If you're not, pretend you are."
—Muhammad Ali

"That man is a success who has lived well, laughed often and loved much; who has gained the respect of intelligent men and the love of children; who has filled his niche and accomplished his task; who leaves the world better than he found it...who never lacked appreciation for the earth's beauty or failed to express it; who looked for the best in others and gave the best he had."
—Robert Louis Stevenson

"A great man shows his greatness by the way he treats little men."
—Thomas Carlyle

"...be not afraid of greatness: some are born great, some achieve greatness, and some have greatness thrust upon 'em."
—William Shakespeare,
Twelfth Night

"The first test of a truly great man is his humility."
—John Ruskin

"Few great men could pass personnel."
—Paul Goodman

"All big men are dreamers."
—Woodrow Wilson

"You have deserved high commendation, true applause and love."
—William Shakespeare, *As You Like It*

"The superior man is distressed by his want of ability."
—Confucius

"To withhold deserved praise lest it should make its object conceited is as dishonest as to withhold payment of a just debt lest your creditor should spend the money badly."
—George Bernard Shaw

Toasts

Here's to your promotion.
Nothing succeeds like success.

If all your marvels one by one,
I'd toast without much thinking
But before the tale was well begun
I would be dead from drinking.

As Dorothy Parker once said to a friend who had just
given birth, "Congratulations: We all knew you had it
in you."

Volunteerism

See also Charity (page 62), Teamwork (page 143), and Community (page 67).

"If you're not part of the solution, you're part of
the problem."
—Eldridge Cleaver

"Life is real! Life is earnest! And the grave is not
its goal."
—Henry Wadsworth Longfellow

"I can't imagine a person becoming a success who
doesn't give this game of life everything he's got."
—Walter Cronkite

"There's only one way to succeed in anything, and
that is to give it everything. I do, and I demand
that my players do."
—Vince Lombardi

"It is our responsibilities, not ourselves, that we
should take seriously."
—Peter Ustinov

Toast

May we be known by our deeds, not by our mortgages.

Here's to doing what must be done.

"I have nothing to offer but blood and toil, tears and sweat."
                                        —Sir Winston Churchill

Voting

Look in Politics (page 118) for more material.

"The ballot is stronger than the bullet."
                —Abraham Lincoln

"Voting is the first duty of democracy."
                —Lyndon B. Johnson

"Bad politicians are sent to Washington by good people who don't vote."
                —William E. Simon

"Whenever a fellow tells me he's bipartisan, I know he's going to vote against me."
                —Harry S. Truman

"If the ballot doesn't work, we'll try something else. But let us try the ballot."
                —Malcolm X

"Nobody will ever deprive the American people of the right to vote except the American people themselves."
                —Franklin D. Roosevelt

"Vote for the man who promises least; he'll be the least disappointing."
                —Bernard Baruch

"If you don't vote, you're going to get a spanking."
—Madonna

"A straw vote only shows which way the hot air blows."
—O. Henry

Toasts

May those who don't vote never complain.

To the miracle of changing governments without war.

Here's to those who fought for our right to vote.

Weddings

Weddings, showers, rehearsal dinners, and all the related occasions have more complicated politics than a national election. Accept it, and don't get involved. This is not the time for you to bring attention to second cousin Rosalee who wasn't invited. It's also not the time to remind the crowd of the horrible things that were done to your people by the neighboring people back in the homeland.

Your job as a speaker or toaster is to say something nice about the bride, or about the couple. Keep it brief. Avoid the temptation to talk at length about yourself and your feelings and what might have been.

Look at Love (page 102) for more material.

"Never above you. Never below you. Always beside you."
—Walter Winchell

"Music played at weddings always reminds me of the music played for soldiers before they go into battle."
—Heinrich Heine

"Marriage is a community consisting of a master,
a mistress, and two slaves, making in all, two."
>—Ambrose Bierce

"Look down you gods,
and on this couple drop a blessed crown."
>—William Shakespeare, *The Tempest*

"All mankind love a lover."
>—Ralph Waldo Emerson

Toasts

Here's to you:
May you live as long as you want to,
May you want to as long as you live.

Here's a toast to love and laughter and happily ever after.

When children find true love, parents find true joy. Here's
to you two, may your joy and ours last forever.

May you two grow old on one pillow.

These two, now standing hand in hand,
Remind us of our native land,
For when today they linked their fates,
They entered the United States.

Here's to the bride
And here's to the groom
And to the bride's father
Who'll pay for this room.

Down the hatch, to a striking match.

To the happy couple: May all your troubles be little ones.

As Shakespeare said in Romeo and Juliet, may
"A flock of blessings light upon thy back."

May their joys be as deep as the ocean
And their misfortunes as light as the foam.

Last Minute Speeches and Toasts

Here's a toast to love and laughter and happily ever after.

Here's to the new husband
And here's to the new wife;
May they remain lovers
For all of life.

May your wedding days be few,
And your anniversaries many.

Index